The Binman's Guide to Amazing Customer Service

Top customer words, service concepts & interviews to help create a sales focused customer-centric environment that provides amazing customer service.

Oisín Browne

@binmansguide

The Binman's Guide to Amazing Customer Service *Top customer words, service concepts & interviews to help create a sales focused customer-centric environment that provides amazing customer service.*

This edition is published by Book Hub Publishing.
For further information: www.bookhubpublishing.com

Printed in Ireland
Cover Design by Ray McDonnell
Edited by Dr. Niall MacGiolla Bhuí, TheDocCheck.Com

First Edition

ISBN: 978-1-9160883-2-0

This publication is designed to provide accurate and authoritative information in regard to the subject matter covered. It is sold with the understanding that the publisher is not engaged in rendering legal services or other professional services. If legal advice or other expert assistance is required, the services of a competent professional person should be sought.

The author and publisher state that all writings in this book are the suggestions and views of the author and accept no responsibility for the outcome of any suggestions applied.

To buy The Binman's Guide to Marketing, The Binman's Guide to Selling & The Binman's Guide to Amazing Customer Service in bulk contact the publisher at info@bookhubpublishing.com - The books are ideal for your management team or as a corporate gift for your clients, suppliers or partners. Special discounts are available on quantity purchases by corporations, associations, businesses, networking groups, universities, business schools, sales teams, agencies, and for seminars.

Praise for The Binman's Guide to Amazing Customer Service

"Oisín's book is a true gift that shows us how to celebrate our customers." **Shep Hyken**, *Customer Service and Experience Expert, New York Times and Wall Street Journal Bestselling Author*

"Browne shares real-world tips and practical ideas from his 20 years of experience working at the front line of The City Bin Co., an award-winning company known globally for its outstanding customer service. With the theme on company culture and creating a customer focused mind-set this book is a must-have that will give you an edge with your valuable customers." **Verne Harnish**, *Founder Entrepreneurs' Organization and author of Scaling Up (Rockefeller Habits 2.0)*

"Oisín Browne's book is more than just a buffet of effective service strategies; it is a call to arms for a relational approach to customers. Browne has created a powerful resource for people at all organizational levels to help them not only deliver better service but also to develop deeper customer relationships." **Adam Toporek**, *Customer Experience Expert and Author of Be Your Customer's Hero*

"This is an enjoyable introduction to improving your game when it comes to delivering amazing customer service. If you want to bring the best out in your employees and provide the best service to customers, this is your book!" **Jeanne Bliss** *Best selling author, 5-Time Chief Customer Officer, Customer Experience Pioneer and Leadership Advisor*

"Oisín has put together an amazing collection of tips and techniques aimed at helping you improve your customer service and experience. Now, it's up to you to dive in, rummage around, pick a handful that resonate, implement and practice those til you are at them. Then, you should dive in again and repeat. That's the way to greatness. Oisín has given you the tips and the ideas. Now. It's up to you." **Adrian Swinscoe** *Best selling author of How to Wow and aspirant CX Punk*

"How companies communicate with customers, particularly the language that is used, is an often-overlooked aspect of customer experience. Browne provides an important read that will pay immediate dividends to your business." **Dan Gingiss**, Customer Experience Speaker, Consultant and author.

Contents

Ten Amazing Customer Service Words that Matter

Delivering Amazing Customer Service starts with you

Amazing Customer Service is delivered by those who look after their people and develop their culture

Amazing Customer Service is the new standard for your amazing customers

Amazing Customer Service happens when you turn the complaints into compliments

Meet the World Class Customer Service Experts

Foreword

Before you begin reading, I would like to add one small tip of my own to Oisín's book. It concerns a question I cover in my latest book called; *The Convenience Revolution*.

How easy is it to do business with you?

The customer's experience must be joyful, easy and convenient. I truly believe that being more convenient for your customers is the best strategy when it comes to improving customer experiences. Any add-ons, changes or upgrades to your offerings need to make the customer's journey seamless and convenient for all the right reasons. Too often, we hear how important it is to put yourself in your customer's shoes. This is correct, but how exactly do you go about that? Within the pages of this book you will find the answer. This book is a treasure trove of tips and techniques that will improve your customer's experience through better employee engagement, culture, training and systems that bring consistency to you and your team.

When Oisín sent me a draft of this book, I loved its simplicity and format. The language is accessible and makes the book very easy to read. It is full of customer service anecdotes, tips and suggestions that will give you new ideas to apply to your business or position. You'll want to dip in and out of the chapters. It is a really useful companion for anybody starting out in a new job or business. It will reinforce good practices, teach you some new ones, and help you focus on delivering excellence to your customers. Out of all the ideas and inspirations that you will read about in the following pages, start with one that resonates with you and put it into action. Then move to a second idea, and a third. You get the idea. There's plenty to work on.

Finally, without giving too much away, the thing I love about this book is how Oisín encourages us to celebrate our customers and our employees. Customer service must be a joyful experience for everyone involved. Oisín's book is a true gift that shows us how to celebrate our customers.

Shep Hyken, *Customer Service and Experience Expert*, New York Times *and* Wall Street Journal *Bestselling Author*

Preface

Welcome to the third offering in the Binman's Guide series of business books. The first book covered the basics of selling and put down an excellent foundation for the mind-set needed to win at selling. The second book was an overview of the marketing landscape and provided a solid understanding of the world of marketing. This third book focuses on providing amazing service to customers.

When I first started writing these books I knew it would be more than one book. Although it wasn't the first book I wrote I knew that the Amazing Customer Service book would have to happen. I know that the focus had to be more than *just* customer service. It had to be *amazing* customer service. I remember when I was reaching out to interview companies for the *Selling* and *Marketing* books people were happy to contribute, but would tell me straight out that the *Customer Service* book was the one that they were waiting for. In many ways, it's apt that this book comes after the Marketing book as I truly believe when you deliver excellent customer service, you feed that success directly into the marketing efforts that, ultimately, drive your sales. You 'wow' customers with an amazing service. That story is told by the consumer and creates an interest amongst potential customers.

To deliver amazing customer service with stellar support, the overall focus must not be only on the customer and the service, but on the employees, culture, values, mind-set and attitude of the people representing the products and brands. It doesn't matter if you work with customers on the front line or in sales or marketing, in an office or in management, you are part of a team that needs to make the customer's journey an amazing one. I hope through sharing my thoughts, ideas, experiences and stories obtained over two decades working in this environment that you get inspired to **up your game** and make the service you deliver or the job you do or business you own one hundred times more customer focused and amazing.

Every business provides customer service, some bad, some good and a few exceptionally outstanding. We all have had amazing experiences that surprised or wowed us. We have had the experience where we shake our head and say, *'never again'*. Sometimes, when we have that *'not so good experience'* you can have an amazing turnaround of events where the people you are dealing with cultivate the right systems and empower people in place to make your experience what it should be. Nobody ever gets it right all of the time but I believe the following tips and techniques will help you to get it right most of the time. And, if it does go wrong, the right things will happen to right that wrong. More than ever, amazing service is expected in today's business environments and I believe when you provide amazing service to your customers you can put a price on it. This book can be summed up in one line: **People will be happy to pay for amazing customer service**. Let's be to the forefront in providing this experience.

Oisín Browne

Introduction

The Binman's Guide to Amazing Customer Service is the third book in the The Binmans's Guide series, following on from The Binman's Guide to Selling (2013) and The Binman's Guide to Marketing (2016). In many ways, The Binman's Guide to Amazing Service may be seen as the crescendo as The City Bin Co. was literally an experiment in customer service.

When Glenn Ward and I founded the company in 1997, we wanted to see if it was possible to bring service excellence to a very traditional industry – waste collection. An industry known for many things, but never amazing service. Thankfully the experiment worked. Our first tagline was *'the difference, is our service'*. The implied difference was the difference between The City Bin Co. and all of the incumbents.

These days practically every company promises 'amazing service' but very few actually deliver. Trying to operationalise amazing customer service day in and day out requires a culture and mindset that only the most disciplined of companies can deliver. Amazing service happens long before the customer steps into the picture. Amazing customer service happens deep in the design on the business, it's not an afterthought or an optional extra.

However, as you will see in the following pages, amazing service need not be complicated. In fact, as Oisín will show you, **amazing customer service is about being big on the little things**, about keeping things as simple as possible and, most of all, about being able to **walk a mile in the customer's shoes**.

Finally, I will leave you with my most important business lesson. It's impossible to give amazing customer service on a consistent basis, for over twenty years, without having amazing people. Thank you Oisín and all your colleagues – past and present!

Gene Browne, CEO, The City Bin Co.

Get the best from this book

My intention with this book, as with all my books, has been to share ideas and inspirations that will get you enthusiastic about what you do professionally and encourage you to do small things that will affect your work and business in a big way. The focus of this book is to give people getting started in business and people already in business a ton of tools that they can take to help them be better at providing amazing service to their existing and potential customers. In this book, I decided to focus on the people in the business and the systems and mind-set that they can have that makes a big difference to those they are servicing. *Customer Service* comprises of two powerful words that mean so much. I really believe it's about the culture of the company and the attitude of front line heroes delivering that all too important service. The small things like eye contact and smiles matter. Follow-up and listening without distractions make a difference. Building techniques and learning from peers are essential when providing the best to customers. Do you have a learning room or learning meetings within your business? If so, you will learn from every experience. You will need to gather that information and share the learnings and apply best practices if you wish to improve your service and offerings. If something really wowed a customer. Listen to that customer and test if what wowed that customer is being done consistently for all customers. When you see amazing conduct from a colleague or somebody going above and beyond on your team - point it out. Let everybody know. Cheer for your Peers. Peer recognition is fuel for the whole team to make a better effort. If you get only one thing from this book that changes the way you provide a service or deliver a product that makes a customer's experience an amazing one, I will be happy. Sometimes, **we only have to move the needle a fraction to have an impact**.

As with my first and second book, this book is intentionally written in a way that permits you to casually dip in and out at any point. Open it at any random page and start reading the chapter you choose. It is written to inspire creative thinking that can be applied to your business activity to help improve the overall experience of your customers. No matter what position you have in your company or where you are in business, it is always helpful to have somewhere to draw additional ideas from to help you give the best possible service to your customers. As always, this is your book, so write on it, add to it and highlight the parts that you find interesting and useful. Enjoy the read and if there is something in here that you think may work in your delivery of amazing customer service, do it. Test the waters and if it works, roll it out!

Ten Amazing Customer Service Words that Matter

While working at The City Bin Co. for many years, I never felt like I worked for a waste collection company. We were never excited about waste or trucks or skips. We were exited about the customer, service and experience. This was the culture instilled in the company. Founded in the late 1990s, the company pledged to provide excellent customer service experiences to an industry where it wasn't expected. You could say the customer focus culture chose the words, but the words defined the culture. As far as I was concerned, I worked for a customer service company that happened to collect waste. Our daily duty was to provide amazing service.

The words you use everyday can build bridges between your company and customers. They can prevent and recover your customers' experience from disappointment while creating a customer-focused culture. Using the right words can make a memorable first impression. Establishing strong values amongst employees from the outset will encourage them to get the job done right and will give your customers something positive to talk about. Amazing customer service acts as an anchor that can help reassure customers and employees. When you say what you are going to do before you do it, you give the customer a sense of trust. Today's customer will recognise the scripted waffle and marketing jargon that was once standard place in business. They can tell if what they are hearing is said with integrity. Be honest. Be real. Be you.

Identifying the right language can have a positive impact on customer relationships. Words are tools to communicate. The real substance is in the energy, enthusiasm and certainty of the words being said. Anybody can rhyme-off a line, but if there is no heart behind what you are saying the customer will sense it. Speak with clarity. Use words to empathise and to centre the conversation back to the subject matter if it goes off topic. Be prepared and be sincere.

I am not going to say that by using these exact words everything will be fantastic. You need to add your own touch of magic. You will know words that work better for you. Let this book be your starting point to inspire your next conversation and transform a typical customer interaction into the excellent experience.

1. Thank you

How it works

Being thankful and understanding of the customer's time and their belief in your company means that they will part ways with their hard-earned money. A **thank you** can be as simple as 2 words, and it can be so much more. Gratitude can be equally expressive when there are no words, such as a simple smile. Follow-up by email to ask if the client was happy with the product or service or if anything should be better. It can be said with a gift, for example, an eBook or a how-to video. The most important thing is that it is said with sincerity and heart.

What to say

Some airlines are amazing at this; think of when you disembark a plane after a long flight. Cabin crew thank each person exiting the plane. I was getting off my Emirates flight from Dublin to Dubai on the 3rd of April 2017. I was really impressed with how the airhostess waited at the door as everybody left and said **thank you** to each and every customer. They say it with eye contact and a smile. It's warm and well mannered.

Always schedule a follow-up meeting, be it one day, one week or one month later. This is one of the best ways to say thank you. Follow-up immediately after a sale with a meeting, a handwritten thank you note or a courtesy call to see how everything is going for the client and to show your appreciation. Every time any of The City Bin Co. Sales team sign up a new customer, they reach out exactly one week later. Firstly, they put it in their calendar. Secondly, they meet the new customer face-to-face or, if this is not possible, they will call them. It's an opportunity to say thank you and make sure everything is going well for the new customer and build the relationship. When your customers interact with your business online, whether to submit a form or make a payment, you could link each transaction with thank you note. Too often, we send a receipt or invoice overlooking the **thank you**. Remember, don't just thank your customers; say thank you to all your staff and suppliers. They are your soldiers that show up every day to make business happen. Thanking your employees shows them that their dedication and efforts are noticed and appreciated, giving them a good reason to go the extra mile. **'Thank you' is a timely loyalty builder.** Start building.

2. I agree

How it works

When a customer is expressing a complaint or a tribute to your service or product that you genuinely agree with, support them and let them know this. Speak clearly, as the words can't be denied; *'I agree'*. By agreeing with the customer, it means you are on their side. Listen to their needs and reassure them that you will work on their behalf to solve any issues or to pass a compliment to the responsible department or person.

What to say

The expression **'I agree'** is a short, simple and effective bridge of harmonisation between you, your company, the customer and most importantly their experience with your product. It is especially effective when you close it off with a follow-up conclusion statement or action plan.

For example, if a client is unhappy with your service and explains why they are dissatisfied, or the service falls short on your product promise, you can show empathy by saying:

*'John, **I agree**. I will change this right away to make this work for you. I will also take steps to change our process internally to make sure that the error doesn't repeat'.*

*'Mary, thanks a million for sharing your experience with our service. You said it is really good that you received a text message saying which bin to put out the next morning. **I agree**. I have sent your feedback on to the team that collect your bins'.*

When a customer buys your product, sometimes it's because they have an idea or expectation of what they will get from your company. Most times that expectation comes directly from you. If this was not met and you agree, let them know.

*'Niall, **I agree** with you. When this company started over 23 years ago, it was established on the foundation that we would change the industry by providing a great service. Thanks for highlighting the issues you are having with our product. You have reminded us of why this company was first started. I will act immediately to make sure you get the service that you were expecting'.*

3. Feel, felt, found

How it works

The feel, felt, found strategy is used in customer service to manage a concern from a client who may have a grievance with your service. The three sections of the strategy are: To identify with the way the customers **feel**, to convey that others (or you) have **felt** the same, and to share what changes or solution they (or you) have **found** to fix the situation. I learned this technique from Anne Cooke, who has worked in The City Bin Co. customer centre for over 10 years.

Empathise with the customer. If you have shared a similar experience or you know of another customer who had an experience similar you can express that to the client by sharing the solution. This confirms that you are listening to the customer. You share the similar experience that you or another customer had and then you share how you or that other person overcame the problem or the solution you used.

What to say

*'Hi Karen, I understand that you **feel** disappointed because you are having problems logging into your account. I **felt** the same when this happened to me after I signed up to the service. What I **found** worked best for me was to change the password so an email will be sent that will enable you to reset your secret password to an easy to remember secret code. Let me show you and we can walk through it together'.*

The idea here is to connect with the client so they don't feel like they are alone or that they are the first to have this problem.

*'June, I understand how you **feel**. Initially, John, another determined salesperson, **felt** the same way. John **found** that by cleaning up his pipeline every day, there was less confusion and his work was more organised, allowing John to get more done. I believe it will be the same for you'.*

*'James, I know how you **feel**. I had a new member last week who **felt** the same way as you do. She **found** that after coming to the classes the routine became a habit. Once this happens, it becomes so enjoyable. The more you do it, the more it will become second nature to you'.*

4. How can I be of service?

How it works

Noel Kelly, a mentor and business friend with whom I share an interest in sales, taught me to ask in every business interaction: **'How can I be of service?'** At the end of the day, that's why you are in business. You want to help. There is no better way to cut to the chase and find the relevant solution for the client by asking this question. Most times, the customer knows what they need better than you. Guide them with your expertise but only if you know exactly what is needed.

The giant supermarkets and retail outlets of the world know this. Every time I'd enter the Carrefour outlet at the Mall of Emirates in Dubai when doing my weekly shopping, I noticed all the staff wore t-shirts with *'Can I help you?'* printed on their uniform. They didn't just wear the words, they practised them by being proactive in helping customers find items and answering questions about different products.

What to say

When you ask **'How can I be of service?'** you acknowledge that the customer is present and that you are there to take care of their needs immediately. Some people are shy and may not know where to begin. It is always easier for you to lead the discussion. This simple interaction refocuses the conversation.

*'Good morning, Sir, My name is Sam. I see you are browsing the different products in our showroom. If you have any questions, let me know **how can I be of service**. I will be more than happy to help'.*

This phrase is useful when seeking more information about the customer's requirements.

*'Hi John, This is Oisín from The City Bin Co. I received your email enquiry this morning. **How can I be of service?** Tell me about the quantity and type of waste you produce on site'.*

5. Definitely, surely and certainly

How it works

When researching for this book, I started at the core of The City Bin Co.'s customer centre. I sat with the amazing customer centre team as they answered incoming calls. During that time, what stood out was the ability to listen and reassure the customer using a minimum amount of words with maximum impact and to allow the customer to express themselves uninterrupted until all the facts and relevant information had been articulated. When I spoke to Anne Cooke, at The City Bin Co.'s HQ, she said it's important to let the customer know you are listening without breaking their flow of communication. For Anne, using the positive 'ly' ending words such as 'definitely, surely, certainly, absolutely, and exactly, allow her to do exactly that. The words can anchor the conversations.

What to say

There are a set of words that end in 'ly' that can add a small bit of positive support and backbone to your conversation when used on their own to indicate you are attentive. Some examples are: definitely, surely, certainly, exactly, absolutely, and there are many more. Also, when placed in your response you add positivity and strength to your commitment.

'We *definitely* will make sure that your skips get collected today'.

'I *absolutely* agree that the right action here is to send a representative out to visit so you can get a first-hand look at how the machine operates and how to best keep it maintained'.

'I can *certainly* help you with your request and I am happy to do it right away'.

'*Certainly* John, I will look into this right away and get it sorted. I will notify you once everything is done'.

There are so many 'ly' words; especially, exactly, delightfully and speedily are some of my favourites. The important factor no matter the words is to really put your heart behind what you say.

6. My commitment to you

How it works

Too often when it comes to amazing service, the word *commitment* is missing. This is the one thing we give when selling and marketing but not enough of it is given after a sale. An important part of the customer experience is you and your companies' commitment to be by the customer's side all the way. It may not be possible to be physically present all of the time, but to give the commitment that you have the right processes in place or the right people available should the need arise is crucial. The follow-up on this is essential to providing amazing service. If there is an issue with a product or a customer feels short-changed you will win back their trust by having a strong follow-up. The best way to do this is to give them a clear upfront commitment that if anything isn't what it should be, or they need a little guidance, here is how it can be obtained right away.

What to say

Don't just give a commitment. Say it with commitment. Say the word commitment. Nothing carries the meaning of the word more than the word itself. It's powerful. When you give a commitment to the customer you are giving them 100% attention. You are being honest and upfront with all what you are going to deliver in terms of your next agreed action.

*'John, Thank you for contacting us today with your issue in regards to your purchase. **My commitment to you** is to find out what is happening with our service at your location and get back to you with a solution within the next 20 minutes'.*

If there is a problem with the product or service, acknowledge the issue first and then make a commitment to resolve it.

*'In relation to what you just told me about the service you were provided I understand your disappointment. This time we didn't get it right. To avoid a similar inconvenience in future, **my commitment to you** is to send you out a voucher for the full value of the service so that you can have the experience that you deserve'.*

7. I'm sorry...

How it works

If the company was wrong in any way or the customer was let down, the best move is the simple step of putting your hand up and saying **I'm sorry**. To say sorry is to take responsibility. There are numerous potential circumstances in which you may have to apologise to a customer. Sometimes, you have to refuse a request or simply can't provide what you promise because of some unforeseen circumstance. Maybe a customer was on hold for a little too long on a call or you got their order wrong. Saying **I'm sorry** is vital to demonstrating your duty to deliver. It says; I'm human. It's humble. Instead of going through the motions of why something did or did not happen it's better to deliver a genuine and effective apology.

What to say

You can waste so much energy on justifications and excuses when, often, the customer just needs to hear a simple and heartfelt **I'm sorry**. These words can be the bridge between the customer's problem and your solution.

*James, I'm calling you regarding your email dated 21st of March 2017. Before I explain the reasons leading to this unintended mistake, I would like to sincerely apologise to you for any inconvenience this may have caused. This is clearly a mistake from our side. **I'm sorry** and take full responsibility'.*

*'Sue, customer happiness is something we genuinely value. Unfortunately, sometimes the inevitable happens and there are mistakes. In such rare cases, a satisfactory solution is always in place and preventable measures are introduced, however, I want to say **I'm sorry** for any inconvenience caused. I am here with you to make this right'.*

Or it can be as simple as: *'Ronan, I messed up. **I'm sorry** for the inconvenience that you have faced. what I can do for you now is ...'*

*'John, I have no excuses. Firstly, I want to start by saying **I'm sorry**. Secondly, given the opportunity let me explain exactly what I will do to make this work as it should have in the first place so you can have the experience you expected'.*

8. May I?

How it works

It can be difficult to tell a customer what you need to do without coming across as patronising, especially when dealing with complaints. Yet, incorporating a phrase such as '**May I**' into your language can help you to overcome this and create a more positive customer experience.

'**May I**' is about giving a sense of ownership to your customer. It's a polite permission based form of conversing.

What to say

Using a soft phrase like *'May I'* to start your conversation or request can help you lead the conversation to a more positive outcome.

*'**May I** help you?' and 'How **may I** help you?*

To get some time to gather facts and figures you might say: *'Ray, **may I** take a moment to investigate where exactly the roadblocks with the service are and I'll return with a solution once I have gathered all the correct information. Is that fair?'*

May I is useful when you want to vocalise what you are going to do before you do it. It acts as an upfront agreement.

*'**May I** repeat your order to make sure everything is correct?'*

*'**May** I suggest switching off and on the device when it is fully charged?'*

*'**May I** take this opportunity to thank you for your interest in using our service and bringing this to our attention?'*

*'We don't carry that product on our shelves, however, **may I** recommend an alternative product you can use that will give you that same result?'*

*'**May I** conclude our conversation by summarising the next action that I believe will put you in a position to have a positive outcome?'*

9. Follow-up

How it works

Follow-up is the one thing that wins the sale, solves the problem, and makes things happen. When a customer is not happy or a sale didn't happen or there was an error in processing payment, generally it was because you didn't follow-up. The biggest complaint that I have seen in customer services is dealing with clients disappointed with poor follow-up with their original inquiry. They need to re-explain their issue when calling back and sometimes have to repeatedly contact the company to get their issues resolved. As a result, they are likely to speak poorly about the company. They will go onto tell people about their bad experience. The solution here is an upfront agreement on the **follow-up** with the client.

What to say

The best way to **follow-up** on any outstanding task is to commit by vocalising to the customer who's going to do what and when it's going to happen. When you say this, you make a vocal contract to take ownership for completion of any actions pending. You are responsible.

Say it to the client and follow it up by email. Also, take responsibility to make sure the follow-up happens even if you are not the one doing the direct fix. You are the one accountable.

*'Niall, To **follow-up** on your inquiry I will file your request and then I will organise a new distribution for you. As soon as I have the details, I will text you the time and date of your delivery'.*

*'Robert, we will **follow-up** with your product delivery so you don't have to. As soon as the application is completed, we will contact you and let you know'.*

Also, it's important to be proactive where possible and contact the customer before they contact you. This will allow you to pick up on any shortcomings in your service and put out any flames before they can spread.

*'Hi John, I am calling you today to **follow-up** with you on our products you have been using over the last month. How is it going for you?'*

10. Happy to help

How it works

Most customer service interactions can be broken down to the basic: 'I have a problem' and 'Let's fix that problem for you'. The use of positive words and phrases can help relax both parties. To do this successfully, a phrase I like to initiate such conversations is: *'I'm **happy to help** you with this'*. Using this positive tone can essentially change the way the customer sees the experience.

By using positive words, you can make your customers feel more positive. You are making yourself available to be of service.

A modest approach like adding this positive power phrase to support your interaction can make a big difference. Noel Kelly of Argro plastics once said to me *'Business is all about helping people, to be in business is to be of service. If you can't be of service, you are not in a healthy business'*.

What to say

When a customer calls you about a difficulty that they're having, instead of responding with *'I'll look into this for you,'* say, *'I'd be **happy to help**'*. People, in general, don't want to bring up problems or to be a burden. They might think you don't care. It's your responsibility to find out if they are happy with the service or product. It's your job to find out if there are issues to be resolved from your end. The best way to open this door of communication is to tell customers you are **happy to help** with anything good or bad and that you are always available to hear them out.

*'Bob, Let me know if there's anything else I can do for you. I'm **happy to help**'*.

*'I am **happy to help** with any concerns that you may have. Please tell me how things are going for you?'*

*'Harry, I want to thank you for sharing your situation with me. First thing I want to say is that I'm **happy to help** with this matter so that your experience can be improved to what you originally expected'*.

Delivering Amazing Customer Service Starts With
You

Delivering amazing customer service starts with you, your first impressions, your delivery of the service or product, the quality of the product, your follow-up and how you respond when it goes right and when it goes wrong. You cannot control the actions of customers nor their reactions to service, price or product. What you can control is your approach, your presentation, your manners, your tools and systems, daily disciplines, employee engagement, ongoing training and overall positive culture and conditions that you work in. Customer service is too often only seen when things go wrong and if you don't have the right tools and skill sets in place to follow-up, correct and learn from any experiences that don't go your way it can have a serious impact on the bottom line.

Customer service means so many different things to different businesses. The easiest way to look at it is to look at the two important words; Customer Service. The customer and the service. That's what matters. What can you do to make the overall experience for the customer amazing? and what can you do to improve the service or product that you provide? In this fast-paced world of consumerism things do go wrong and people do get wires crossed and unforeseen situations do happen. It's not what happens that highlights good or bad service to customers but how you proactively respond to what happens. Good outcomes can be pure luck occasionally but to get amazing outcomes and provide amazing service every time you must have a job done mind-set, reduce bottlenecks within your product delivery and have the right people with the right daily disciplines, tools and tone. This starts with you, the one providing the amazing service and being of service. Be one hundred percent present. Be one hundred percent respectful. Be one hundred percent engaged. I believe when you focus on raising the standards within the team this is reflected in the experience of the customer. Giving an amazing service is about dedicated people making a smooth delivery and after service of a particular product, which gives a positive experience to the customer. You have to be responsible for your role in making it all happen. The following pages are guidelines and motivations for you and your business to wow your customers with amazing service.

11. Make an amazing first impression

How it works

Making an amazing first impression is all about leaving the right lasting impression. This is achieved by good preparation, knowing your customer, presenting you and your product in the right light and listening effectively with a view to being of service to the customer. Also, know the people within your company that have the power to make a strong first impression.

When giving an amazing first impression it's not just about the response. The appearance and willingness of the people meeting customers, those responsible for answering the phones, responding to emails and social media platforms all play a part. It stretches across every point of contact in your company. At The City Bin Co., the real heroes responsible for upholding its reputation are the frontline personnel who collect the bins and skips every day. They do it no matter what the weather throws at them. They get up early in the morning and they clean the streets. They say hello to passing strangers and they wave and smile at kids. They focus on the little things such as putting bins back in the correct locations and making sure that they are well-mannered and attentive on the job at hand.

What to do

If you want your customers to experience, talk about their experience with you and become repeat customers you must change the way you start your conversations and interact with them. I'm not saying to be different, but to be more excited and attentive. Treat every follow-up interaction with the customers with the enthusiasm you would if it were the first. There are many elements to making a first amazing impression from dressing well, being positive, being on time, having the correct information required on hand for the customer and good follow through. The ultimate goal is that no matter what is going on with the customer, be it a sale or a complaint, you must make the customer feel relaxed and comfortable and confident that you can bring a resolution to their problem or close the sale in a way that makes them feel good about their interactions. This all starts with you.

Start with your place of work and practise good manners, friendly greetings and honest conversations. Promoting the right culture amongst colleagues and business peers will positively influence their interactions with the customer. This must happen with everybody from the ground staff up to top management. Identify the people that are at the frontline and facing your customers every day. Let them know they are important to your business. Train them. Give them the tools needed to be responsible and presentable. Show what is expected in terms of displaying good manners and having a customer-focused attitude when in work or off duty and whether they are speaking with customers or friends. First impressions are given by all employees, both customer-facing and background office, support and operational staff. In the waste industry, it's the workers collecting the skips. In a coffee shop, it's the guy at the till taking the orders or the waitress cleaning the tables. In a hotel, it's the receptionists and the housekeeping staff. These are the frontline heroes. They give the first and lasting impression through their work and their ability to communicate well with customers. Who are the heroes in your business?

12. What's your name?

How it works

Chester Santos '*The International Man of Memory*', famously said, '*When you can remember somebody's name, it shows them that they are important to you*'. When James Kent and I walked into the bar of the Sheraton Hotel at the Mall of Emirates in Dubai in October 2016 we were both impressed with the hotel host. He was an Egyptian gentleman by the name of Abdou Hassan Gharby. As we entered the bar, Abdou shook our hands and made good eye contact. With a warm smile, he said '*Hello Mr. James and Mr. Oisín, Welcome back. It's so nice to see you again*'. We were both amazed because we were only ever there once before and that was the previous June when we stayed at the hotel for a few nights on a work assignment. Abdou makes it his business to know everybody's name and to welcome them.

The power of learning, knowing and addressing your clients by name in business has many positive outcomes, such as repeat business, familiarity, good rapport and respect. The customer sees the business representative is attentive and listening, creating confidence between both parties. It becomes easier to address shortcomings and sing praises. This is equally essential for colleagues as it is for staff. This is how you create culture. This is a good place to begin.

What to do

There is the old saying in the world of commerce: 'It's not personal, it's business'. For me, this is not true. All good business is personal and that a personal touch starts and finishes with a name. Your client will either know your name or you will know their name. Firstly, it's up to you to start. Introduce yourself to your customers by means of nametags, verbally introduce yourself and in turn, ask the client their name. Write it down if you have to.

When I was in Doha City Centre shopping mall in Qatar, in March 2017, I went to the cinema to see *Kong: Skull Island*. I arrived early so I decided to grab a quick coffee in Caribou Coffee. I noticed that all of the staff wore hand-written badges that stated their name and which coffee they loved: '*I'm Alex and I love Americano*'. A name provides familiarity and friendliness.

Two weeks later, I found myself in Times Square Shopping Centre in Dubai and I recognised the same branded coffee house. Because of my positive experience in Doha I was drawn to get a take away there and, of course, noticed that all the friendly staff had their nametag and favourite coffee badge. When you learn somebody's name and a little something about them you build trust. This trust is the base of any relationship, business or otherwise.

Starbucks is famous for asking the customers their name and writing it on the coffee cups. Each and every time I'm in my local Starbucks in Eyre Square Shopping Centre back in Galway, Ireland, I'm always struck by how the staff ask for my name when taking my order and call me by name when my order is ready. No surprise that some of the staff remember my name and order when I go there.

If you are in an office and communicating by phone always introduce yourself by name first and then the company. *'Good morning, my name is Joe and I'm ringing you from The Print Company'*. You are at an advantage in the office as you can write the name down. If you are not in an office you can carry a notebook or record it in your phone. If you don't know how to spell a name, just ask them. *'Let me write that down. Can you give me the correct spelling of your name?'*

Depending on how busy you are, you might think it's not easy to remember so many names. Some simple techniques to help you remember is to say the client's name back to them a few times within the conversation. Here are a few hacks for remembering people's names:

1. Commit to remembering names
2. Write down their name(s)
3. Repeat the name in the conversation
4. For complex names ask the person to spell their name
5. Associate the name with a visual
6. Focus on the person in front of you
7. Be 100% in the conversation
8. At the end of your day go back over all the people you met.

Mr Abdou from the Sheraton Hotel made it his business to remember the names of James Kent and I. He created a bond resulting in repeat business. What the staff in Caribou Coffee, Starbucks and the Sheridan Hotel have in common is people that nurture great culture. Culture is an established ingredient in customer service. And, for good reason.

13. If you can't be number one, be an amazing number two

How it works

I remember talking to the Managing Director of The City Bin Co. Niall Killilea, when I was looking for advice on a sale I lost. I lost it on price. I had a really solid relationship with the client but they were watching their pennies and I couldn't go any lower or convince them to go with my company and pay a little more for superior service and product. I wanted to push more and win the business. Niall said this phrase to me at that moment, which has always stuck with me, *'Oisín, if you can't be number one, be an amazing number two'*. In other words, let it go. The relationship and respect from the client or potential client is important to maintain. I kept in touch with the client over the years and sure enough within two years, they signed up to our service after a few upsets with their previous supplier.

What Niall said to me all those years ago came to mind recently when I went to the Ulster bank to close an account I had. Branch Manager, Ray Dolan, attended to me. He didn't ask or beg me to keep the account open. He didn't try to make me any counter offers. He thanked me for the business and asked how I was doing and wished me luck. Ray understood and respected that I had made a decision. I was amazed by Ray's warmth, interest and kindness. I know that if I needed any banking services in the future or if my current bank doesn't keep up their level of service, that there is an amazing number two willing and waiting with the doors open.

What to do

If you want to win new customers or win back old customers who choose to leave your service, let them go. That is the only way you can leave the door open for them to come back and do business with you. Always thank them in person where it is possible, for their business and support. Ask them why they are leaving and if there is anywhere they feel you can improve. Wish them luck with their new provider or supplier. Always keep in touch and build on the existing relationship.

14. Start your day with a power hour

How it works

The total opposite of getting nothing done, having too many interruptions in your work, or procrastination, is productivity. To kick start your day and continue at a top pace, slip a power hour in to your schedule. A power hour is one full hour without unplanned distractions, unrelated phone calls, negative self-talk with yourself or gossip with others, unwarranted pauses for teas and coffee, playing with your phone, surfing the internet on social media and anything else that will stop you from focusing directly on the task in front of you. This is how you clear your inbox. You would be surprised how many emails you can send out in an hour. This is how you call your customers one after another. This is how you clear any back log. When you give undivided attention to any task without distraction you will find that you build momentum and focus as you go further in to that hour. The minute you are distracted you lose the drive that forces you to dive in to the work you are doing and get it done. You lose time. It's very hard to pick up a task with the same focus and energy if you have been distracted. You often go back to the job on hand thinking about whatever it was that pulled you away. The idea of a power hour is that you allow nothing to pull you away.

What to do

It's a bit like swimming in a pool. When you go swimming you swim lengths of the pool. You normally don't stop and have chats or go and make a coffee or look at your phone. You do what you came to do. Swim. This is just like swimming! Look for a quiet time to have your power hour. For me, it's the first thing in the morning. I would even suggest that you wake up early before the rest of the world starts working and get a head start on the tasks you wish to focus on. More importantly, find a time that suits you. This is like an athlete training for an event. When athletes train they are training for results. They focus on one thing only. They focus on their game. It's the same for you. Focus on one task at a time. Whatever is not needed, such as phones or Internet, remove them from your radar. If you work around other people let them know that for that hour you don't want to take any calls or speak to anybody as you are working on something that needs your total focus. It will take time and practice. Print up a power hour sheet that you can monitor the work you are getting done each day and see your progress. You will get results. In fact, I use this method for my writing. And, my editor is delighted with my approach!

15. Follow-up on Friday

How it works

The truth is we should be following up every day. Unfortunately, in today's fast paced 24-hour world it's easy to lose track. After many years working across different areas including finance, sales, marketing, key account management and customer success, I have learned that the most important element of providing amazing customer service is following up. In today's world where the task list can seem unending and overlapping, jobs are continuously left unread in the inbox. It is easy to keep driving forward without looking in the rear-view mirror. You have to make sure nothing is left behind. That's really the idea behind follow-up Friday. It's to double check the week as it comes to a close and use this check list as an opportunity to check in with the people you connected with. Depending on the volume of calls and task and meetings it may not be possible to touch base with everybody but you can take the time to do a scan of the weeks event and reach out with a quick message to the top 10 clients with whom you communicated. When you finish a follow-up Friday session you end up with a **Freedom Friday** allowing you to start the weekend with the past week completely closed off.

What to do

Why do this? To take stock and set yourself up for a fabulously productive week ahead. It's a discipline that helps you get super organised and it's an awesome thing to do. Yes, it takes planning and time. But the pay-off is efficiency and possibly more business as you build the relationship with your customers. Start by following up on all your week's interactions. Use your calendar to go back over all the meetings you had, calls you made, messages you sent, leads, proposals and anything else where you had an interaction with a customer. **Close the loop with gratitude**. Thank them for their communication and where possible give them a one line recap of the interaction. For me, I use *Salesforce* and set up task reminders on a daily basis to remind me to do a quick recap at the end of each day and every Friday, for one hour I will review the week and contact the people I met to wrap up the week. The result is that the communication is always received with gratitude and sometimes it triggers the receiving party to request products which creates new business.

16. Develop daily disciplines

How it works

To create a customer focus culture within a company, develop daily disciplines that will help deliver the best and most seamless experience to the customer every time. Creating this in your culture will enable you to perform at your peak and measure your success daily. You create a consistency within your work implementation. Creating these disciplines produces a pulse to your performance. Daily disciplines start with you. They are the few little things you do everyday that have a big impact on your customer's experience. It's a bit like brushing your teeth or making your bed. You don't have to do them but doing them will have a significant impact on your comfort and health. In fact, peak-performance guru, Tim Ferris includes making the bed as one of his five morning rituals for winning the morning. In 2014 at the Commencement address at the University of Texas, Admiral William H. McRaven spoke about the daily discipline of a Navy Seals trainer listing one of the first tasks that should be done as 'making your bed'. Now, I am not saying making your bed will make your customers happy unless you run a hotel! I am saying instead, start the day well and continue with the same awareness and appreciation that allow the simple habits to become a regular part of your routine.

What to do

Do a daily diary of each task that is carried out within your company by you and your team. Map your day. Look at your meetings, internal and external communications and KPI's. Make a commitment to give importance to the small things that you might pass up on if you are too busy. Identify what is important for you. It might be a tidy desk, morning huddle or daily updates. When I was on the sales team at The City Bin Co. I would jump onto a conference call every morning to give my daily statistics. Nobody would ever be late to the call. If I was in a meeting I would step out for 2 minutes knowing that's how long the call takes. The calls were a daily discipline. Every new customer receives a new welcome pack. This is a daily discipline within the culture of the company. Before leaving each day, I will systemically plan out my calls and customer visits for the next day. These were small things that made life easier for both me and the customer. Figure out what daily disciplines take a small amount of time and energy to get right. And for the love of humankind, if you want a productive day, make your bed!

17. Deal with the distractions

How it works

Managing your time effectively can be challenging in today's world. We live in a state of continuous distractions from our smart phones with instant notifications and social media channels that allow users to scroll endlessly through pictures and videos of people we do not even know. It is easy to be sucked in and go from one end of the day to the other and achieve very little. If you arrive at the end of your day and the work is not getting done you have got to look at you time management. You must delete the distractions or block off time for 10 minutes during your break to look at these distractions. **Control the distractions or the distractions will control you.** A distraction at work can be anything from the above-mentioned interference from the digital world or a colleague or a stranger sapping up your time telling you stories that go over time. Stories that can wait, instead, for a break. There is no harm in a little short chitchat once in a while so long as it does not upset the flow of work or cause the work to be delayed, delivered badly or left undone. Distractions are sometimes a bad excuse to not do what we should be doing, working and reaching our goals and taking responsibility for our role which contributes to better customer interactions.

What to do

To deal with distractions you need to become selfish with your time. You need to block off you calendar and stick to the agenda. Everything else can wait. You must get comfortable with saying: *'No, not right now, let's take this offline'* or *'I am busy with back to back tasks, let's talk about that later'*. Switch off any notifications on your digital devices that may interfere with you work. Put your phone on silence or airplane mode and turn it faced down when working on a project or task. Create strict boundaries about personal phone use and full blown conversations about the earth, moon and sun when working. All the updates will be still there on the phone at your break or when you clock out. Shorten the small talk. When somebody wants to share something that's not work related you can acknowledge their conversation and ask to hear more later. For example, you might say *'Emily, I really want to give you my full attention. Why don't you tell me about it in more detail over a coffee at break time'?* You could also address your commitment to work by simply saying, *'I am busy right now, let's catch up later'*. You are saying the conversation is important, but right now my work is my priority.

18. Sharpen your time management skills

How it works

I used to think that *'time management'* was something that stopped me from doing things my way. I used to love to let the day plan itself. I was convinced that this gave me a freedom and ability to move with a flexibility that gave me an edge. I found out the hard way that this is not true. When I went from working in the small City of Galway in the West of Ireland to the fast-paced City of Dubai in the UAE, I simply had to change. The City was bigger. The clients were bigger. The contracts were bigger. The distance between meetings was longer and the company where I worked was a huge international company with many departments. Ultimately, I knew if I was to work well, I needed to get organised. I had to stay away from distractions, make a schedule and stick to it. When you take on more and more tasks without organising them into a daily schedule you can create more chance for things go wrong. Following up becomes poor and undone tasks can cause sales to be lost. The purpose of sharpening your time management skills is to free up time and control your work flow in order to get more done. It is the process of planning your time spent on particular activities in order to increase your efficiency and productivity.

What to do

Start improving your time management skills by organising your days and weeks in advance. One way to do this is to write out every task and activity you do day to day. Look at repetitive tasks, short-term and long-term tasks that can be astutely prioritised according to goals. Instead of looking at your emails every hour or when they arrive in your inbox, spend a limited and planned hour reading, responding and sending emails. Detach yourself from social media. If it is essential to your daily task then schedule a half an hour to review your different platforms. Prioritise your tasks and do not allow for disruptions. Set boundaries with your tasks by controlling your environment. Place your phone on silent and switch email notifications off when they have nothing to do with the task on hand. At the end of the day look over your calendar and see what tasks were achieved without distraction. Leave an hour once a week that you can allocate to the good and bad distractions. Great time management eliminates procrastination. Learn to delegate where applicable. Learn to say no where there is no fit or relevance to your scheduled task at hand. This can be hard, but practice is the only way to get comfortable with saying 'no'.

19. Don't confuse 'important' with 'urgent'

How it works

Stress levels can become high and overwhelming when you have an unmanaged list of tasks to do with more tasks randomly added as you try to complete them all. I have been guilty of having a 'to-do list' that rarely got completed. It was always frustrating as, many times, urgent and important jobs would get put to the back of the queue leading to overdue deadlines not being met and customers waiting too long for something to be resolved. The Eisenhower Matrix helped me to take control of my 'to do' list. I first learned about the Eisenhower Matrix when attending a 'Time Management' masterclass in the Middle East. The Eisenhower Matrix was conceived by General Eisenhower before becoming President of the United States. When he served as general in the army during World War 2, General Eisenhower had to make fast decisions and hard choices about which of the many tasks he should focus on each day. This led him to create the world-famous Eisenhower Matrix, which today helps us rank and schedule daily incoming tasks by urgency and importance. In 1998, Stephen Covey adopted the idea to create a time management matrix detailing them as 4 quadrants.

What to do

Covey said, *'The key is not to prioritise what's on your schedule, but to schedule your priorities'*. Instead of just making a 'to do' list or marking everything in your calendar. Start with the priorities. Mark every task with one of the following 4 categories:

1. **Do immediately** the most important tasks that are **urgent** and will have a big impact on completion.
2. **Schedule** the **important but not urgent** for that or the next day.
3. **Delegate** what's **urgent but less important.** People like to help and many hands make light work!
4. **Don't do** what's **not important and not urgent.** These are the tasks that should not be on your radar.

This matrix addresses the relevant activities related to your daily objectives and core goals. You must prioritise them over activities that might demand your time but are less important and not urgent. Stop doing the activities that steal your time and energy every day. It will help you keep your eyes on the prize.

20. Have a 'job done' attitude

How it works

To have a job done attitude means to have a 'can do' attitude. It means to take ownership of whatever task is in front of you and make sure that it is completed professionally, speedily and correctly. Simply put; pull your weight at work. When you have a 'Job done' attitude, you don't put things off for a later date that can be done now. You don't give it to somebody else to do. You take charge of it until it's marked **job done**. A positive and enthusiastic approach is a critical component and the success of a job done attitude in the work place. It needs to be embedded in the culture. If it doesn't come from the top down and you are not at the top, **force positive change upwards**. C. S. Lewis, a famous British author, once wrote; *'Life is 10% of what happens to you and 90% of how you react to it'*. This quote is very true in the work environment. I'm not saying you should do everything and be a 'go for it' or a drone doing everybody else's job. I am saying know what you have to do and do it well. And if you get some tasks from left of field, own it, especially if there is a customer waiting on the other side.

What to do

Identify what kind of job attitude you currently have. Ask yourself if you like to put off until tomorrow what can be done today. Maybe you are a lazy person or easily distracted. By knowing how you work today it's easy to set goals and simple rules for yourself in relation to how you will react in the future so to make sure to have a job done attitude. No pain, no gain. Don't take shortcuts. Don't pass a task on to somebody else. Put in the hard work and take responsibility for the job that you do, the company you work for, or own. Get regular feedback from your colleagues and customers to identify what you need to improve to have a more job done mindset. Intentionally, put yourself into situations that allow you to practice new skills and give more value to the tasks and customers on front of you. Always show up on time and always know what you have to do. But don't just show up. Show up and shine bright. Be seen. Be proactively engaged with all the customers.

21. Keep your work space clean and tidy

How it works

A messy desk screams stress and a lack of organisation. I am guilty of having an untidy desk at work and driving a car where the passenger seat is a big mess with papers, notes, envelopes, notebooks and phones, pens, newspapers and empty coffee cups so scattered that it's next to impossible to find anything. You might believe you have no time to tidy up and need to get on to the next task or that you'll do it later. The fact is it takes two minutes to stop and arrange what's on front of you. The merits of doing this is that it is professional and projects an aura of proficiency and know how. It's something for you to be proud of. It's no different than dressing smart. It creates an impression. Once you know where everything is you will work more efficiently.

What to do

Take five minutes before you start your day and when you end your day to clean your space from top to bottom. You are responsible for your work space. Make it so impressive that when people pass they think wow! Putting items where they go produces less clutter and better work flow. Check your digital space. From time to time, clutter can sneak in and hijack your desktop too! Do you just save everything to your desktop until you have icons from one side to the other, making it pretty hard to find anything? Create four or five folders that are relevant to the work you do. At the end of the day get in the habit of tidying up the files and putting them in the applicable folder. Be sure to name your files and folders correctly especially if you share them with others. See your space at work from the point of view of an outsider and think about what it says about you.

22. Break the rules

How it works

When it comes to delivering amazing service, you got to break the rules! Especially if the rules do not make sense. Too many services are running so tight that they forget the most basic thing. Customers are humans and are all different. Somebody might want something not on the menu. If you have the ingredients in the kitchen then do it. Do they want extra onions? Say yes. An awkward request, say yes. If you are afraid that their request will become the new norm educate them for next time or consider if something is being requested that causes you to go outside of your normal offering, change the product! Give them what they want. The customer will pay if you do. You will pay if you don't because they may choose your competitor next time. If there is a better way to do something that will make life better for you and your customers then do something about it.

What to do

Set a protocol to follow. This is the right thing to do until it is not. Rules and guidelines help a business ensure quality and maintain a certain consistency of service. Most businesses have rules in place. What they don't have in place is that one rule that says this exceptional circumstance calls for a deviation from the everyday rules. If you are the owner or manager, be accessible if somebody on your team has a better way or sees a small win to make an experience better for a customer. Empower them to do so and make the channels of communication open, easily accessible and responsive. Having this mentality helps you make the right choice when keeping customers. When you are tied down with rules and procedures you can do more damage to your business in terms of what the customer expects or deserves. I am not telling you to break the rules if it damages the company's reputation or goes against the values. I'm saying if you have to bend the rules because it will add to the experience do it. One of The City Bin Co. 's principles is: **If you discover a better way, shout!** This principle empowers all employees to break the rules when there is a better way. If it is something that needs top management approval which most time there is too much off anyways, write it down, present it to the management team and ask them if you can trial your idea and return with the results. If the results show your way as saving time, energy and money or improving customer satisfaction at a high level, ask for a full implementation.

23. Stretch like a cat

How it works

Sitting in an office with your head tilted in the same position for long periods of time can add a large amount of pressure and strain to the back muscles and spinal discs. People with customer centre jobs or desk jobs generally don't move around much. The tendency is to slouch over time. I used to suffer from back and neck pain when I was working in the call centre many years ago. The cure was simple. Stretch like a cat. Before and after work and at the break times, I would take a few minutes to stretch. Every time I got up, I stretched my arms, legs and back.

What to do

Add stretching to your daily routine and be consistent. Each session should be two minutes every hour or so. If you are not sure about stretching, invite a personal trainer to demonstrate to all the team. My brother Ronan was a personal trainer while I worked in the customer centre and here is the stretching routine he did out for me:

1. Stand up. Slowly reach to the sky and stand on the tips of your toes for three seconds. Repeat three times.
2. Stretch your neck. Move slowly in circular movements five times in each direction.
3. Drop your head down and tuck in your chin. Slowly turn your chin toward your left shoulder, and then slowly turn toward your right shoulder.
4. Stretch your shoulders up to the sky. Hold the position for three seconds and release.
5. Stretch your feet and arms. Reach for the sky while standing on your tippy toes and hold for two seconds and release
6. Stretch your hands. Simply open and close your fist holding all fingers stretched out in the opened position.

This routine was designed for me and we are all very different. Find what works for you. If you have an existing condition or have had surgery then some stretches may not be appropriate. Always consult a personal trainer or professional doctor first. If doing a stretching routine like this isn't your cup of tea simply get up and take a quick three-minute walk. Your body will thank you.

24. Be awake, aware and available

How it works

Too often, businesses are rigid with their opening and closing hours. Yes, it's true, we need a good work/life balance and we need to work to live, not live to work. We do need to switch off. Sometimes, we switch off before the shop door is closed. With that in mind, find a way to be available or use digital platforms to capture and respond to customers. If you have a physical premise don't be so quick to lock the door if there are potential customers wandering around the streets or browsing at your window display.

Over the years, I have seen people who are, what I call, clock-watching. They spend more time looking at the clock, especially between four thirty and five o'clock in the evening when their shift is coming to an end. Once five o'clock strikes, they are out the door like a shot.

The proverb 'The early bird catches the worm' in today's business world means the worm is awake 24/7. Social media and online commerce catch every customer that comes through the virtual doors online. While we can't do the same offline, we can be awake, aware and available where we see possibilities.

When I was in Singapore in September 2017, I wandered around a shopping centre at the moment the shop shutters were going down. I was looking at a travel MIDI keyboard through the window of the Swee Lee music store that had a closed sign swinging across the door. Within two minutes, the door unlocked and the lights went back on. Sean Tan and Edwin Chian were on the evening shift that day. Sean invited me inside. I told him I was only window shopping and thanked him. Suddenly, I was inside talking to the two gentlemen and making a purchase. Because they stuck around for an extra ten minutes, they made a two-hundred-dollar sale. These guys were clued in to their potential customers and they created an experience. They delivered an amazing service by sticking around and opening a door that had been closed. All three of us left the shop smiling.

What to do

So, what do I mean by 'awake'? **To be awake** is to be focused without personal disruptions. I have walked into many shops to find shop assistants deep in conversation with their friends, texting or engrossed in their mobile phone. Basically, being distracted and unaware of their surroundings.

To be aware is to have a radar for existing and potential customers with the sole intention of being of service to them.

To be available is to be approachable and welcoming. If you have a traditional walk-in premise, stick around for five or ten minutes extra. Turn your mobile on silent and leave it out of sight when you are with a customer. Nothing is more important than to be in the present moment.

When my wife Eva worked in O'Connor's Bakery in Salthill, a seaside resort in Galway City in Ireland, she would often get a few passing customers after she closed the shop. She stuck around to serve them and would use the extra time to prepare for the following morning. These late arrivals would become regular clients over time.

25. Be an amazing listener

How it works

They say to be an amazing listener is the trick to being a great salesperson. When you truly listen to somebody who brings you a problem, two things happen. Firstly, you solve the problem faster and secondly, you relax and reassure the person with whom you are speaking.

What to do

The only tools you need are your two ears. However, you have many other instruments that stop you from using these to your best ability, such as your thoughts, impatience, and other pending tasks. One way to address this is to only allow yourself to respond with gratitude. A simple *'Thank you for sharing'* is one of the most powerful replies to show you are listening.

I attended a workshop based on the book *The Five Dysfunctions of a Team* by business consultant Patrick Lencioni. One of the team-building activities required every member to state the best and worst thing about each person on our team. The only response allowed was 'Thank you'. It was difficult in the sense that I couldn't ask why or defend myself when every person on my team described me as impatient. Saying thank you to everyone was rewarding and honest. This exercise forced me to listen and accept what was being said to me. Another really useful habit is to ask questions to draw out more information such as, *'Tell me more,'* and *'What outcome are you expecting from this conversation?'*

When addressing a problem or dealing with a disgruntled customer, use the Five Rs to conclude the conversation in a positive way.

The Five Rs are:

1   **Request** more information on the client's issue
2   **Repeat** what they said back to them
3   **Reassure** them you will help resolve the matter
4   **Resolve** the interaction be telling them exactly how you are going to fix the problem and the timeline involved
5   **Restore** the relationship by scheduling a follow-up call for some time after to make sure everything is back on track

26. Be only in the present

How it works

One morning in February 2019, I received a very impressive calls from the CEO of Frank Byrne's Auto Repair Service. I had called to Frank's office the previous day to leave my father's car in for repair. I have known Frank for years. He is always one hundred percent focused and present in his business. I was delighted to see him and that he was able to accommodate me in servicing my dad's car. The car was booked in for a service and I didn't think any more of it until the call from Frank the following morning. Frank called me to apologise for not giving me his full attention as he was focused on something else. I felt as always, I had a super interaction with Frank but I was so impressed by his own self-awareness and respect for each of his customers that he called me up to say that he wasn't fully present in that moment. I was amazed. It also prompted me to write this chapter as I believe Frank is an example to all business people. You will never see Frank looking at his phone or on his computer when you speak to him. He will give you his time and full attention with eye contact and follow-up. That evening, Frank stopped to assess how present he was and felt it could have been a bit better although I have to admit if every business person gave half of what Frank gave me that day we would have an instant increase in delivering amazing customer service worldwide! To be present takes effort and discipline and this only comes with practice and acknowledgement of short comings and successes. In many ways, it's up to you to set your own bar. Aim high and fall high. Be like Frank.

What to do

Assess how present you are and recommit to being more present. Look only at the present moment. When you are present you have better meetings. You will get more done. You will increase your productivity and problems get solved with more accuracy. Sounds so zen but it's true. Focus on the past and you can get caught up in things you can't change. Focus on the future and you fill your head with the 'if's and buts' of every scenario that has not yet happened. When you focus on something else in the room other than what you need to be focused on or the person whom you are with, you may not take in all of the conversation. Be aware of the moment you are having, with whom you are with and how much of your mind is present. Just do one thing at a time. Don't look ahead or back. Be present. When you drive, just drive. Don't be thinking about other things. When you are with a customer be only with that customer. Be present with that customer. Be aware of the conversation, be listening well and be gentle with your response. Set up a daily routine that allows you to have two minutes to reflect on the encounters of your day.

27. Be an amazing giver

How it works

Amazing customer service is first and foremost about giving your customers the ultimate experience. Always remember they took a chance on you and your service or product. Amazing customer experiences when done correctly should bring a positive joy to both the customers, who are the receivers and you, the GIVER. Understanding clearly what you are now. The giver. Start from there. How can you be an amazing giver when delivering your service or product to customers? Your customers can go to a million other companies for the same product or service, so being amazing at delivering your service is where you have to start genuinely giving.

What to do

You don't need to give away the kitchen sink or your profits to be an amazing giver. Write down all the things you can give aside from the product or service. Start with simple courtesy. You can give a smile. You can give gratitude. You can be punctual. You can offer a handshake. You can make all communication easy and convenient. The giving culture is a fundamental part of delivering amazing experiences for your customer. At The City Bin Co. the customer service ethos is so strong that giving is embedded into the culture. There's a free phone number for customers to call. We give empowerment to our customer centre team to make decisions to make the customer's journey amazing. We have dedicated Key Account Managers who are on the road touching base with our customers in real time giving their time to help, educate, solve problems and give an amazing service. We aim for one fix calls. The City Bin Co. have a giving day where each employee is given tokens that can be donated to a charity of their choice. We give follow-up calls to make sure the job has been done well and completed. Give time. Give understanding and give love. Also, everything you give to you customer give to yourself. Giving is very important yet very individual for each company and customer. A good place to start would be to have brainstorming sessions with your team or with trusted customers to come up with new gives that go well with your known brand.

28. Walk in your customer's shoes

How it works

To walk in your customer's shoes is not as hard as you might think. You do it everyday. You are a customer to others and this is the best place to start walking in your customer's shoes. Being a customer is a normal part of your life so take time to observe other professionals when you go shopping. Focus in on that. If you want to give amazing customer service, go out and learn from the experiences you have when you shop every day. When you are buying a coffee, or doing the weekly shopping in your local supermarket or buying something online, start by being conscious of the services and after service offered. Take notes on what you like and what you don't like. Ask yourself if this was done within my industry with my products how would it add value. Having this mind-set allows you to benchmark outside your industry and commit to continuous improvement. To be an observing and learning customer helps you see the world from the point of view of a customer. It also helps you improve your services to your customers by applying what you learn from interactions with other businesses.

What to do

This is not about criticising or judging others. You are simply looking to see what you can learn from shopping and using other products and services. Who knows what they're selling that may wow you. Why do they wow you? What are they doing that you don't do? Sometimes it's simply down to enthusiasm or experience. Both of these traits can be developed with consistent training. Look at the manners and the approach of others. Are they friendly? Do they start with a smile? Do they say please and thank you, show respect and listen. Does anybody ask for feedback? Maybe not, but if they were to, what would you say to help them progress? Rate how responsive others are compared to you and your team. Look at the people's communication skills, knowledge of the product and ability to be attentive and assertive. When you shop elsewhere and wish to really see how others perform, be demanding and engaging, but most of all be respectful.

29. Give real-time love

How it works

Is such a chapter needed? Yes, too many businesses rely on third-party companies that do not have the experience or product knowledge, not to mention a lack of understanding of their company's values and culture. Make it easy for your customers to contact you without going through hoops and waiting for long periods. We live in a time where when you call a company you will hear an automated press one for this and two for that. Although the businesses that use this will say it's a system that makes it convenient for the client, it is actually more for the convenience of the company, as they feel they are saving time by directing you to the right department. If it was convenient for the client it would be answered by a person that can help and not a robotic voice recording. Remember, you are there to serve and create an experience. I often find the best route to a fast response is by direct messaging on the social media channels. This is the first place I go to contact businesses. Why? Because this is where I get real-time love. I know I will get a response.

What to do

Never pass the buck or send the customer elsewhere when a customer has a real grumble. They want to speak to you. They should speak to you. Make sure you are easily contactable and work to close off any issues or queries so you create a better rapport with the customer and a better image for your brand. To serve and solve a customer's gripe is to win a fan and a customer for life. Think about what your customers hear when they first call you.

A business providing amazing service will specialise in two important steps in being contactable. The first is to give a clear channel of communication where your customers can contact you easily. This could be a phone number, an email address or social media channels such as Facebook or Twitter. Secondly, if the customers feel like they are having a one-way conversation they will let you know. Be on the other side of the line. Create a flow in your response and have a follow-up process to document the call and close it off in a successful manner.

30. Have a goodwill mentality

How it works

When I was in my early teens, my friends and I use to spend our lunch hour every day in a local instrument store owned by Mike McMahon called Modern Music. Mike wasn't just a businessman. He was a musician. He would not tell us to go or to stop touching the guitars. He'd encourage it by plugging in the amps and handing us the guitars. We had no money to buy the instruments. He knew that, but instead of telling us not to touch the guitars or to leave he treated us as if we were paying customers. The result of this mindset is that, along with my friends, I became a paying customer. Once we could afford to buy these guitars there was only one place to go. Modern Music was where I got my first guitar and all the guitars that followed. This is where I bought my recording equipment. Mike knew the power of treating everybody as if they were a paying customer.

What to do

As my wife says, *'Just be nice, be nice to everyone'*. The first thing to do is to have a welcoming smile and an open door for everybody. Invite people to look or browse. Let the customers sample the goods and try things. If you have a restaurant let the potential customer taste the food.

There is a restaurant on the prom of the port in Javea in Spain where the chef will stand outside when the kitchen is quiet and offer food samples to people passing by. He has no expectations. On a hot day, he lets people sit if they are tired. If somebody enters your space let them be there, touch things and explore. Invite them to ask questions.

If they leave without buying ensure to thank them for their time. Let them leave with an information brochure, product sample or your business card. Give non-paying potential customers something to talk about. When you say don't touch that or think I am not going to give my full attention because they are wasting my time, you are actually saying, *'No don't come here again. And especially don't tell others to come'*. Keep every action with everybody positive.

Where you do find yourself in a position where you feel somebody is overstepping the line take a deep breath, count down from ten in your mind, smile and say nothing. Yes, that's right. Do nothing.

I am sure you heard the saying, if you have nothing good to say don't say anything at all. Treat everybody as a paying customer. Give them your full attention. Be helpful. Be kind and thank them for stopping by.

Ray Walshe from Cara Offices Supplies in the West of Ireland once had a call from the director of a big multinational during the Christmas holidays. He was looking for a place to store his suitcases. As it was the week between Christmas and New Year, Ray knew that most places were closed. Ray offered to go down and meet him at his warehouse, which he opened especially for them. He stored their belongings for a few hours. Although they were not buying anything, Ray was doing what comes naturally to him. He was being nice. The unexpected payback came four weeks later when the director called Ray to thank him for his generosity and to put in a big order to supply all of his offices globally. It pays to be kind to strangers and expect nothing in return. The worst they can do is tell others what a good experience they had.

Successful business entrepreneur Simon Betts told me over a coffee the secret is to tune into your product after it has left the shop. Simon had a mobility scooter manufacturing company in Leicester and Northampton in the UK that he grew from the ground up before it was acquired by the Tandem Group in a deal worth 10 million British pound sterling. An example of Simon's ability to tune in to his product after the sale was when he replaced a mobility scooter for a gentleman who was mugged and his scooter thrown in the canal in Birmingham. Simon came across the story in the local press and quickly reached out to replace the scooter. The goodwill mindset became a positive news story with the local and national press writing about the situation.

Equally, when the programme producers of the Top Gear TV show called Simon to buy two scooters they were testing for a BBC programme, Simon made sure he was available throughout the show when they were looking for spare parts and expert advice. The up side for being available outside of opening hours on this occasion was Simon's product featured on one of the most watched shows on television at the time. Simon told me the backbone to his success was being available and looking after people who bought his products long after the purchase was made. Be tuned into the customer, not just what they are buying but what is happening before, during and after the purchase. Knowing your customer and being kind to them is key to having a goodwill mentality.

31. Lead with your heart

How it works

Using your heart is so relevant in the sale of a service, the experience during the sale and the aftercare of a relationship with the customers. Many old school business expressions have thought us to be emotionless and detached from the customer and the product. *'Don't mix business and pleasure'*. Why not? Real business is about connections and can be such fun! *'It's not personal, it's business'*. Business is very personal, especially as the key to amazing business is building relationships. In business, we are trained to use our head. Without knowing, you work from a base of fear, the fear of not doing the right thing, the fear of losing the client or not winning a customer over. And the fear of losing a job or not getting a promotion. This way of thinking can kill enthusiasm and destroy company culture. The key to eliminating the fear that kills a good work spirit is to empower the employees to work from their heart. This is the secret to elevating a company to proving amazing customer service. When you lead with your heart and know that nobody is looking over your shoulder with a rule book you can give more of the following to customers:

- Time to listen and empathy to their situation
- Flexible solutions to individual needs
- Elevated enthusiasm and acceptance of all outcomes
- Commitment to the customer

What to do

Make a decision to connect with your customer. If you are telling yourself you are a transactional company only focused on the money you are not an amazing customer service company and you are not leading with your heart. When I say **lead with your heart,** I am saying to look into your customer's eyes and be one hundred percent present about their need for your service. Be of service. Let them know you, not just as the sales guy or customer service call centre person. It's about being open to suggestions. It's about empathy. It's about knowing what to do to make things work. Michael Gerber, American business author and entrepreneur, once stated; *'To use your heart in business is not about you and it is not about me. It is about the act of creativity; that "sudden seeing" of a possibility we have never seen before'*.

Amazing Customer Service

is delivered by those who look after their

people and develop their

Culture

32. Understand company culture

How it works

It's tough to define culture in business. If I had to boil it down to one thing I would say: **Culture is established by the attitude and behaviour of the leadership of a business**. You could say; change the leadership and you change the culture. I believe this is true, but unless you have a set direction guided by a strong leader, you could be swopping out one bad egg for another. Company culture isn't just one thing. Yes, it's guided by the leader of the organization but it is so much more. It is the character of your company. It's the collective personality that the customer sees. It's the vibe. It represents the environment in which you work. It's the backdrop of your business. Company culture can be created using a variety of elements such as a company mission, values, ethics, expectations, and goals. These are nothing if you don't have the right people, space and atmosphere. It's the empowerment of you and your colleagues to do what needs to be done. It's your buy-in and fit to the company spirit. It's your daily interactions and sincere passion about what you do. Amazing culture promotes collaborations and rewards successful initiatives. Amazing culture listens and respects different opinions. Strong cultures celebrate their history and have a strong relation with their customers. In a letter to his entire team in October 2013, Airbnb's Brian Chesky defined culture as; *'Simply a shared way of doing something with passion'*. Author of Organisational Culture and Leadership, Edgar Schein, states 3 ways to understand culture: Firstly, **Artefacts**; the visible things like what people wear to work or every desk is a tidy desk; Secondly, **Beliefs and values**; which are more invisible, like respecting opinions and decisions; and thirdly, **Basic underlying assumptions**; which are usually oblivious, like a belief that you should hire people like yourself or a principle that no product or service should be given without review. While the day to day running of the business will bring you all sort of issues and problems such as financial strains and product pressure points, they will all pass. What will always be evident is the culture. And a strong culture will solve any problem and unravel any issue with more ease and faster than an uncultivated culture. *'Culture eats strategy for breakfast'*, is a famous phrase coined by management guru Peter Drucker and made famous by Mark Fields, President at Ford. I believe both are important and that there is a direct relationship between a healthy culture and a company's strategy which, in turn, affects profits. That said, culture is a tough thing to balance. It's a moving target that has different values to different people. It's something that grows and evolves over years.

What to do

To understand your culture, you need to evaluate your current organisational culture. This can be done by electing a Company Culture Officer (CCO) who's task it is to oversee and implement a culture strategy. They need to look at the people. Interview the employees. Look at the space. Are the offices well located and divided? Look at the tools, phones, computers, wall displays and TV screens. Look at the canteens, washrooms, parking and common areas. How do people use these spaces? Are they welcoming? Look at communication. How do you communicate with your colleagues? Is there a positive atmosphere in the business? What interactions do employees have inside and outside the business? Then look at the company from the top down. Does the management team or the CEO embrace transparency? Are employees appreciated and rewarded for valuable contributions to the company? Is there a social club or a team events manager to nurture strong relationships between colleagues? Is there empowerment on the front line and is this supported? Is there flexibility? Does the company communicate the values, goals and purpose? Are they understood and delivered with passion? It's important to display and communicate core values to all members of the team. When a new employee starts at The City Bin Co. they attend an introduction workshop with the CEO of the company to introduce them to the company history, values, customer expectations, mission and purpose. This is the beginning of creating a high-level trust between the leadership and all members of the team. It demonstrates open communication. As a main driver in The City Bin Co., culture-learning ranks high with opportunities for career development, mentoring and training provided through programmes such as *'Earn as you learn'* and *'Garbage University'*. There is no 'one fits all' solution for creating culture but there are a few basics that can be achieved from the get go, one step at a time:

- Create an environment of trust
- Respect all employees and customers
- Communicate your core values and principals to all
- Empower employees by allowing them to make decisions
- Embrace failure. Make an acceptance for mistakes and risk taking
- Encourage creativity, innovation and the development of ideas
- Collect feedback and suggestions
- Create a learning environment where the team can grow together
- Measure success by the mood of the camp and not just the sales, KPIs or a P&L sheet

33. Celebrate your employees

How it works

When we reward employees, we celebrate their giving of themselves to the company. A lot of people go to work day in and day out, year after year with the only acknowledgement of the work they have done being their weekly or monthly take home pay. I am not saying to acknowledge bad habits or poor work productivity. I believe there are two basic things to award. The first is time given. When you or your colleague has passed the 1 year, 5 years, 10 years or 20 years of service - give gratitude for that time. Understand that time is the most important thing you or anybody can give to a service, product or project. Yes, everyone gets paid for the work but if you give gratitude for the time you will get far more back in terms of work, dedication, more time and, most importantly, a happy worker which, in turn, equals happy customers. Now you might say why reward somebody for time as they may not be a great overall contributor? Well, I would argue that the minute you give gratitude for the time served you will find that commitment levels rise. I remember when I was a young boy how proud my father was of a wooden clock with a stone base that he had placed in the centre of a mantle piece over the fire in our sitting room. He was presented with this clock to mark his 15 years of service with Steiners, a German factory which he worked for another 35 years until his retirement. It's very simple. When you reward people you are saying to them; *'I see you and I thank you'*. The second basic thing you can reward you and others for is exceptional service or working beyond expectations. This sets a standard. It shows others what can be done. It helps the average to step up and be an A player. As a young 17-year-old, I took my first job in McDonalds. Every month, there would be an employee of the month. Every time I would work a little harder, a little better in the hope of being the next one. A company with an amazing culture doesn't just award the employees, they celebrate them. The winner each and every time: **The Customer**.

What to do

Reward yourself and your employees. Decide the timeline or milestones that should be celebrated. Think about the reward. What is it? Does it show gratitude and appreciation? It could be a certificate or a beautiful trophy. It could be a picture. Don't just give the award in passing or mention it on the company blog. Do all that and celebrate it. Think about having a special moment to mark the occasion. It could be a night out or a simple lunch for the team. There is no price on the return a company can get for an expression of a gratitude. An acknowledgement of an employee is a positive message of appreciation.

34. Identify and look after your frontline 'heroes'

How it works

Take advantage of your best placed assets: Your front-line heroes. These are the people throughout every business that are the faces of the company. They see the customer every day, speak to the customer, serve the customer and know the customer by name. These are the first points of customer contact or in some cases, first point of an after sale contact. They are the receptionists and cleaning staff in hotels, the delivery drivers, baristas and waiters in coffee shops, cashiers and floor staff in supermarkets, the guys on the back of the bin trucks picking up the trash. They are the employees who are closest to the actual service. They have a frontline view of how the customer is engaging your brand, product or service. In most cases, the product cannot be delivered without them. Everybody else; finance, IT, admin, management and all the other departments are there to support these frontline heroes. Frontline heroes more than not sit at the lower end of the structural hierarchy of any business causing their first-hand observations and opinions to be ignored. However, the reality is that this is the best data building point for any business wanting to provide amazing customer service. These are the people who will see in real time the happy customer or the frustrated customer. They know when business is low or when footfall is more than usual.

What to do

Identify the frontline heroes in your company. Talk to them. Learn from them. Help them grow and learn within the company. Learn what information they can bring back from their customer interactions that can build customer profiles, improve customer reach and build stronger relationships that trigger repeat business.

Get the right tools for the frontline heroes. I have seen first-hand companies that make sure that senior management all have the newest model phones and best laptops, yet the valuable front-line sales teams who are calling customers day in and day out and who need to enter data on spread sheets have the cheapest models. If you are at the front line make sure you have the proper tools for the job.

Train your team to grow and excel at their front line by running scheduled monthly events. Include role play scenarios, techniques, industry case studies and guest industry speakers who can share experiences and tips. Implement what you learn. Keep what works and kill the ideas that don't help.

Collect daily feedback about the interactions with customers. Think numbers. How many customers do you interact with. How much money is made? How many customers did not buy or did not return. This helps to create real targets and spot patterns when there is a change in customer behaviour.

Empower the employees at the front line to operate independently. Granting customer-facing staff the authority to make fast decisions in their customer interactions builds trust and allows them to deliver amazing customer service.

35. Display your achievements

How it works

When you display your achievements, awards and certifications in the right space, you are sharing precious moments with your customers. You are placing reinforcing triggers for you that you are an achiever and you have standards to adhere to when delivering your service. It shows credibility to the customers. It helps to build confidence in the brand and it is a powerful first introduction to a company. That is exactly what happened as I awaited to enter my first of many meetings with Christian Zaiden, Director of Environment, Health & Safety for the Rotana Hotel Management group at their head office in Abu Dhabi, UAE for the first time. I was waiting in the reception as I had arrived 10 minutes earlier. I took 2 minutes to go over my notes and spent a moment looking at their display of achievements, everything from best-managed hotels to quality certifications. It became the starting point of our meeting. I paid a compliment to Christian on the awards and the display. It was a positive opener to the meeting.

What to do

Awards or certificates placed prominently give a good impression of quality, responsibility and standards. Display everything you have won or been awarded. Remember to check the date and put the latest achievements at eye level. Talk about awards and achievements with your customers, partners and suppliers. Enter as many awards as possible; you may be surprised at the results. Look for awards and courses that are relevant to your business or sector or values. Use the achievements as a sales tool in brochures, on your website or when speaking to potential clients. It's a great conversation starter. When I introduce The City Bin Co. I don't just say I represent the company. I say I am part of an award-winning team that provide an amazing service. At The City Bin Co. Head Quarters in Ireland anybody entering the lobby is greeted with a wall of awards and achievements that have been won down through the years.

36. Cross train with colleagues

How it works

The City Bin Co. famously run quarterly themes that encourage and facilitate the growth of the company through various tasks called *Quarterly Themes*. In Verne Harnish's book, *'Scaling Up'* he talks about the success of a particular quarterly theme ran by the company in January 2012 entitled *'180 to One'*. There were 60 employees at that time working with the company. The idea was for each of the staff to job share once a month with another colleague in the business. This would equal 180 days of cross training in the company over 3 months. I experienced it first-hand when I was working on the sales team. Each month, I would job share with a colleague. In the first month, I sat with the accounts apartment. The second month, with the front-line heroes on the bin trucks collecting the garbage and during the third month I spent a day in the recycle centre. I got a great sense of the different roles within the company, how what I did and how well I do my job effected others. When you walk in the shoes of others you learn to appreciate their roll and they learn to appreciate yours. The end result is a better functioning team that works with more consistency and efficiency to serve the customers. The team building exercise builds trust between team members. When the sales team walks in the shoes of the person delivering the service or goods and the accounts person answers calls in the call centre, it builds an appreciation and trust which help shape that one important element needed for amazing customer service, **culture**.

What to do

Create a monthly plan to outline each role within the company and to indicate who is going to swap tasks or sit beside a colleague for a day each month. Identify the roles and tasks for which cross-training is needed. Establish targets for tracking the success of the plan. Start off with some achievable skills that can be easily explained and taught to others. This is a solid way to build team confidence. Explain to all the members of the team the reason for cross learning and the benefits to the people participating and the company as a whole. Schedule adequate time for the training. Supply any training materials, and training facilities in order to make the tasks a success. Think long term. Create a completion and reward plan for members of the team who satisfactorily complete a certain number of months cross-training and can demonstrate their new understanding of a different role or new skills learned.

37. Help colleagues under pressure

How it works

When the sleeves are rolled up and you feel you are going against the tide it can mean a lot when somebody says, *'Can I give you hand with anything?'* Be supportive and conductive of a team spirit. Amazing teams understand that the collective effort will influence the end goal therefore providing a better service. In most cases a little applied pressure can bring out the best in productivity, however we are not all built the same. People respond differently to distinctive levels of pressure. For some, it is a catalyst to perform at their best and for others it can be a curveball that throws them off course causing them to lose their everyday focus and work ethic. For the accounts team, there can be the pressure of running the invoices at the end of month. For sales teams, there is targets to meet and if something stops the service from happening such as a webpage that is down, an employee that didn't show up or vehicle that is out of service, everybody can be effected. It's at this time when a colleague reaches out to help that deadlines are met and pressures are eased. A colleague dealing with a crisis will always welcome someone taking an active interest, providing some guidance or helping with the heavy load.

What to do

To overcome these moments of pressure there are two qualities required. Firstly, that each person brings their best self to the game in terms of abilities that will help achieve the goals or tasks on hand. This simply means plan, focus and execute. Put the phones on silence and kill all interferences. Secondly, proactively support colleagues in those moments where it may be hectic. Sometimes, if somebody has a hundred tasks to complete, a colleague offering to take ten of the tasks can release the pressure. If your colleague is working to a tight deadline with no time for lunch, offer to order them in a pizza or salad. Make sure you and your colleagues have the resources needed to do good work. Also, in times of pressure challenge your colleagues to keep up. Encourage them to the finish line. Although everybody has their own roles and jobs, if we work in silos without looking at the guy in front of us or behind us we fail in the whole idea of being a team. Helping colleagues is not the norm but it's a stand out quality in any team when the ship is hitting rough seas. When the pressure is on always remain calm. Start by planning and prioritising key tasks. If you are under pressure let people know. Ask for a little help. It goes both ways.

38. Create a 'praise your peers' platform

How it works

My first job was at the McDonalds Drive thru on the Headford Road in Galway, Ireland. It was in my forth month there that I learned the value of recognition when I received employee of the month. It felt empowering and I felt part of the team. Employee peer recognition is one of the best building blocks in creating an exceptional long-lasting company culture. Everybody has people on their team that does their job so well it allows you to do yours exceptionally well also. Often times, we are too busy with our day-to-day tasks and may overlook a colleague that goes that extra mile. Companies with peer recognition programmes can address this with a simple 'Thank you' bullet-board in the workplace. Even though peer recognition comes from co-workers, the benefits for the company and customer are enormous. More than management, your peers have the unique perspective to view the work you do and see how you contribute to the team. They see your attitude towards the customer and company and can measure your readiness to serve the customer. Giving praise to your peers builds a strong team spirit among colleagues resulting in employees to focus on the common goal of servicing the customer.

What to do

Create a 'Praise for your peers' platform. Make it user-friendly. There are digital platforms that use this tool but you can start with a dedicated email address where the team can sent email praises that list the name of the person they wish to praise, the action of that person and the time or day this action happened. Make the praises visible. When you post the positive praise in a place for viewing it becomes a powerful tool that encourages better work productivity and creates positive peer interactions. When you put peer praises at the forefront of your culture you open channels for better communication. Be inclusive and have no limits on what is recognition. A praise is simply acknowledgement of somebody who went above and beyond. It is an all-encompassing method within your business that creates powerful visibility for the attitudes, behaviours and contributions that make your company function. Praises create new norms and standards. Create a monthly top recognition prize, a praise for peers committee may select one recipients for some achievement or you could set a threshold number of praises automatically qualifies for special prize.

39. Rate your days, weeks, projects & meetings

How it works

So many systems, surveys, performance measurement tools are over complicated and ask too much questions. They are not goal driven. They are answered by the manager. They are abandoned or they give the wrong data. The best example of touching the pulse of a company in terms or people, sales and culture was during my time working on the sales team in The City Bin Co. At the end of our weekly call every Friday, the team would rate the week. They would give one number. It was their number that took into account everything from their work and personal life. Their weekly performance and overall wellbeing. It is a simple formula that allowed everyone to give quick honest feedback, which would identify problems and create realistic goals on an individual level with the support of the team. If I ask you, *'How is your week going?'* I will properly get a cloudy answer such as *'okay'* or *'fine'* or *'good'*. If I ask you to rate your week I will get a number, an honest answer. If your week was full of distractions and full of difficult tasks, the number could be low and, equally, if you had a good week the number might be high.

What to do

There are many platforms to help you and your team rate your day, week, month, meeting, event or project. Some examples are TinyPulse, HappierCo, Teambit and many more. If an application isn't your thing, simply commit to rating whatever you want a collective feedback on between 1 and 10. If it's a meeting, include it as a short meeting in your calendar. There is no need for long meetings. It can be done by email. It can be done face to face or by dialling into a private online call. It only takes 2 minutes. Don't go into long sad stories. Keep it short and to the point. The first question that needs to drive the performance, goal or project is: **How would you rate your day or week between 1 and 10?** The second question is: **In one line say, why?** And with minimum words, question three: **What one action are you going to do to improve or maintain that number?** Creating consistency and accountably within one's performance is key to achieving positive results. By allowing yourself and your team to do a self-appraisal you bring responsibility into the equation. The results focus on the number and not the stories or excuses. It's target driven. It's supported and realistic. It's measured and quickly points out shortcomings when targets are not reached. It's fast. It's honest and it works.

40. Create company mantras

How it works

We all have good and bad days. Days that go well and days where you just want to give up because it feels like everything is going wrong and it can be tough to get back on track. These are the days where a few simple and effective words repeated over in your mind can give you the space needed to deal with what's on front of you. When you repeat something over and over to yourself, day in and day out, it becomes part of your thought progress when said with conviction and belief. It guides you. Gandhi was once quoted as saying: *"Your beliefs become your thoughts, your thoughts become your words, your words become your actions, your actions become your habits, your habits become your values, your values become your destiny."* This is the essences of a mantra. Mantras are not just for meditation and personal development. They are also a wonderful business tool. *Balsamiq*, a customer focused software company, has six mantras which have shaped the way they do business. Their mantras define their customers and their culture.

The Balsamiq Mantras:

- Help our customers be more awesome
- Genuinely care about our customers' success
- Be good servants' leaders, be good citizens
- Be generous
- Be so good they can't ignore you
- Inspire with our culture

What do do

Mantras are suitable for companies as a whole, or teams and individuals. They are an anchor for the focus of your team. Mantras may be a tool used internally to motivate and focus yourself and your colleagues. A sales team may have a mantra of *'One sale leads to the next'*. A Customer service agent may have a personal mantra such as *'I will solve each case with amazing care and clarity'* or *'I have a job done attitude'*. Company mantras can contain both the cause and result of your success. When I worked with a sales team of a large multinational waste management company in the Middle East where slow payment had been an issue with a number of clients, our mantra was *'A sale is not a sale until you get paid'*.

The mantra focused the sales team on communicating in a different way and setting clear communications on the payment options to the clients when closing the sale. While mantras may not be the ideal solution for every situation they can help align and refocus situations and goals.

41. Start a study session

How it works

In 2013, I was invited to the Etsy headquarters in Dublin by their office manager Jenny King to give a training session on recycling. It was to be part of their monthly *'lunch & learn'* sessions. Every month, they invited somebody from another industry with certain skills that could educate their staff to add something new that could be beneficial on a personal and professional level. That month I was that person. After I gave a presentation, we had an energetic group discussion on applying best practises to the company and also, to their personal lives.

Every Thursday at The City Bin Co., the CEO, Gene Browne sends a weekly *'Garbage University'* newsletter containing everything from his learnings on thought leadership to reflections on business, and current trends. These always included video links, documents and other useful tools. In both cases, it boils down to educating colleagues through sharing knowledge with each other. Senior managers who engage with an in-house learning program where they can read and learn case studies on particular business practices would pass the learnings to their teams. The results in such a practice is a better you and a smarter team that can give amazing service when this knowledge is applied.

What to do

In the professional world of business, we sometimes lack that injection of theoretical training, the books and the new thinking that one might be studying in the university. The main reason is that you are too busy. Set up a best practises session where you and your colleagues can learn and apply the teachings. Schedule sessions for the same time each week or month. Pick a time where you know you will have the most engagement. For instance, some people are better focused after lunch, but not in the hour before. Decide if you will to do the sessions in person, by email or webinar. I believe that sessions should be in person as it is a perfect excuse for team building. A summary of the training can then be shared company-wide. What is the purpose of the sessions? What do you want to learn? Maybe you would like to invite people from other companies to share their wisdom. Spend some time planning out the year. What structure will the sessions take?

42. Get a coffee machine

How it works

At the City Bin Co. we give free coffee to our customers who visit our *'Bring Centre'* when they arrive in with their car and trailers loaded with unwanted material they are looking to get recycled. It's a small gesture and much appreciated by the customers. Most meetings I attend offer a coffee or tea. This is pretty standard practice in a lot of big companies. In the canteen of the Headquarters there is a Nespresso coffee machine. It gets its fair share of daily use with 30 plus staff on site as well as the drivers and workers that will pop into the office and the customers that visit. For the workers, it is a gathering point for networking and time-outs as well as a quick chat. It's a place to catch up with colleagues. It's easy to prepare, easy to drink and always ready to go. I am not going to say coffee is heathy or not healthy. I enjoy a quick caffeine top up in the late mornings. It's a perk to kick away the midday slump. I don't know if it's the caffeine or the break but a nice cup of good coffee is a core part of my routine.

What to do

If you don't have one, get a good coffee machine. A conversation over a cup of coffee builds trust and friendships between peers & cultivates collaboration in the workplace. Invite all workers to use it and when there are any customers in the building offer them a coffee. It's a way to make them feel welcome and as relaxed as if they were at home. Don't give them the coffee while they wait. Have the coffee with them. It shows that you are not in a hurry and are happy to share your time and attention with them. Have a coffee from time to time with your colleagues whether this is in the canteen or off site at the local coffee shop. Here you will build relationships and learn new things. One of the best things about a coffee break is the break itself. It may be only five minutes but you can go back to your tasks refreshed and with more zest and drive to complete tasks. Do respect time. If you have a job to do and only are intent on a quick break, keep it brief. Coffee time for any employee is a break from the daily grind, much like you have adverts on the radio and on Television, the idea in the end is to get back to the show.

43. Start a Sports and Social club

How it works

Business is all about people connecting. The first connections you build aren't with your customers but with your team. Some of the best moments with my colleagues have been at lunch with a pizza or over breakfast in the company canteen. In summer, we have barbeques. There's tag rugby, nights at the racetrack and weekends away involving team-building activities. Friends are made, bonds are developed and problems are resolved.

I was part of The City Bin Co. social club from the day it started. Events are organised by the staff and sponsored by the company. The result is a tighter team who know a little more about each other which humanises their work and colleagues. When you create a stronger bond outside of work, you tend to be more supportive on the job and the pressures that come with it. Creating experiences and memories with workmates builds engagement and motivation. This time translates into better relationships within the business and it directly benefits the relations between staff and most importantly, the customers.

What to do

Social clubs at work can be a fun means of getting to know your co-workers and plan special events for them. If your company doesn't already have one, start one. As much as I don't like committees, this is one place where it works well. Set up a committee with an annual rotation. Plan the first meeting and work out all the details for keeping it running smoothly. The job of the committee is to run the sport and social club and timetable the annually chosen pursuits. Get input from all staff on what activates they would like to partake in. Do an online survey to find out which activities everybody on the team enjoys. Make sure to take minutes of all meetings for the club and that all financial transactions are documented. Plan the year in advance so all the hard work is done. All the meetings, calendar events and projects can be shared. This way there are no surprises and it will be easier to get people to participate. If you are reading this and are the only employee of your company, don't fret. Reach out to other sole traders and small businesses to run social nights once a month. Give the club a fun name and get that logo designed.

44. Sing Happy Birthday

How it works

Who doesn't love to celebrate birthdays or have a simple card to make you feel special? Yes, you are an adult. You have to work. It's just another day you may say, but there is nothing in the world that puts a positive atmosphere in the office with your colleagues like singing 'Happy Birthday' in the best out of tune and loudest voice that a team can muster up! Close your eyes and imagine it's your birthday. Today you're at work, sitting at your desk and the staff around you start to sing *'Happy Birthday'*. Then, your singing workmates hand you a cake and a card with a gift inside. Yes, this is how it happens at The City Bin Co. when it's a staff member's birthday. Everyone gets the *'Happy Birthday'* singalong treatment! Although The City Bin Co.'s birthday tradition is not a big secret, it always comes as a surprise for the birthday person. It is something small and marks a special occasion. This celebration of birthdays is one of the many special perks delivered by The City Bin Co.'s Sports and Social Club that is ingrained in the culture of the company. Celebrating birthdays at work is a proven motivator and the collective mood lifts.

What to do

Firstly, if you are the birthday person and you are your own boss don't worry! Buy yourself a cake and visit your best customer to share a ten minute break to celebrate your day. If you are part of a team, start by taking note of everyone's birthday and put reminders into your calendar so you'll be notified about the day in good time. This is a lovely way to make sure that no one is overlooked. Depending on the budget and time you may want to decide if a quick five minute break to have cake and sing the birthday song will do the job or if something else can be added. Other ideas could include decorating their desk, giving them a gift card, going out for lunch or buying a lotto ticket. Or, maybe just write a simple short personal note from the whole team. If you work in a big organization with a lot of people, as I did when I was based in the Middle East, learn from the wonderful people in their HR department who would have one celebration to mark all the birthdays in the past month. It was always a powerful experience that motivated the team and filled the office with high spirits. You might wonder what has this to do with customer experience or wowing the customers? It has a roll-on effect; happy staff means a more productive team and a positive atmosphere which leads to happy customers.

45. Get social media savvy

How it works

Customer service includes more than the traditional channels by which we communicate such as face to face meetings, talking by phone and emails. Face to face meetings have become virtual meetings with tools such as zoom, skype and google hang outs. Emails are still a big part of customer service but forward-thinking companies are using chat-bots and social media channels to solve customer issues. When it comes to your online activity, there is no black and white. You may work a certain number of hours, yet today's customers are not shopping or looking for services in a 9 to 5 environment. Most of your customers are on social media platforms posting their positive and negative experiences and shopping online 24/7. You have to be there. At the City Bin Co., the customer centre is actively responding to tweets and posts on social media. For them, it is just another channel where they can communicate with the customers.

What to do

Make sure you are set up on all the channels with the relevant information on your products, offering and industry. If you are not in this space you can set yourself up to miss opportunities to interact with customers in real time. As part of the sales team for the company, I would not be involved in posting or answering posts but I would have notifications on any mention of the company triggered. This knowledge is useful when it's something negative that can be acted on in real time and when it's positive to respond and promote. We live an era of fast content and people will post a picture online of bad behaviour such as rude staff or poor parking of company vehicles before addressing directly the people or problem involved. If we are not there to capture these posts, we can't respond or fix the problems. You cannot say; *'It's not my problem'* or *'I am not a social media person'* if it's the company that you work with. You have to position yourself so you are aware of what can and is happening online. If it's a case that you are a small company it is okay to have a message pinned to the top of your channels stating that you will respond to all social media comments, mentions and request between 9 and 5, but make sure you do so.

46. Design your daily basics

How it works

In September 2013, The City Bin Co. started sending daily visuals to each member of the team by email. Each day was a strong short one line sentence reinforced by an equally powerfully message. These images were created by Ray McDonnell, The City Bin Co.'s Creative Director along with the CEO Gene Browne, who came up with the idea after seeing the daily basics chart for another customer focused company in the U.S. called Towne Park. They had a set of values that represented their culture, values and ethos dedicated to each day of the month on a calendar. Ray got the daily '*Cools*' and the images printed up on billboards and placed in the office. It was impressive. It is one of the most powerful internal marking tools I have ever seen. It reinforced the brand. It amplified the culture. Every message was accompanied by a hashtag. *#Cool* and *#Uncool*. This created a new language that the team could communicate. A simple example is if an employee didn't wear their uniform it was easy for their colleague to express this without any embarrassing conversation. It was one word *#Uncool*. Equally, and more frequently, we became accustomed to hear compliments being paid with a simple *#Cool* when a colleague went beyond the call of duty. This was especially evident with our front line heroes collecting the bins, where they would help the elderly, empty bins that the customer forgot to put out, help to retrieve lost property, smile and wave at the kids and endless more *#Cool* examples. The customer experience and focus was already embedded in the culture of The City Bin Co. Now, we had a way to express admiration for the actions of others on our team.

What to do

The idea is to create a collection of simple daily triggers for you and your team that will act as gentle reminders that support your company values and culture. They will help you focus your working day on the best way to deliver your brand and service to your customers. This is not for your customers. This is an internal campaign. Don't try to copy another company's daily basics. This has to be a personal project that represents the personality of your brand at its best. Start by writing a list of everything that you expect to be delivered to your customer outside of the actual product. This could be things like friendliness, punctually or quality. It could reflect your values and purpose as a company. The final number on the list isn't important. What is important is that each one, when read by you and your team, is a confirmation of your company and how you deliver your service to the customer. Think of how you would deliver this daily message. It could be by email or a visual in the workplace. Reflect in the frequency of your message and what might suit. A different reinforcement for each day of the month or you could have seven strong messages, maybe one a day repeated each week. The reason for doing this every day is it creates regularity and is always in sight. If you were to do it once a week you will lose the audience and the message won't be as effective. It gets lost in the crowd of everyday emails and messages. Consider the content. Is it going to be images or text? Set aside a launch date for the project and set the daily basics in motion. This will take time but the key is consistency. Go easy on the eyeballs. Not too much text and soft catchy images. As in the case of The City Bin Co. your daily basics might just influence the language and communication of the organization for the good of the culture and the customers. This is one of the best foundations for balancing the culture across a company.

47. Choose not to do drama

How it works

Sometimes you can't do anything about others who create drama in the workplace, however you can focus on you. While others choose to be happy in a hotbed of workplace drama, you can **choose not to do drama**. No office or workplace is drama-free. When you have a lot of people from a lot of different cultures and backgrounds with emotions and opinions, you can have drama. Drama comes in all forms. The test is to rise above the drama while creating a safe and supportive working environment. Don't engage in drama. Learn to focus on yourself and your work and not others or what they may or may not be doing or saying. If you have anything to say about somebody else speak as if they are beside you or say it to their face.

What to do

This starts with respect for yourself and for others. Your own attitude will determine your response to others absorbed in drama and help you not to get involved in any unproductive or negative dialogues. Don't allow comments and conversations that are simply wrong go without addressing them. Call out bad behaviour and speak up about comments that are rude and designed to hurt someone. Drama left unaddressed is not productive and sends a signal that it is okay to move boundaries. Boundaries are there to help people work well together. This is done through respect. When drama enters the room, comfortableness and confidence in your work can suffer. To stop unwanted drama you must speak honestly to the people at the source of that drama. Lead by example. Focus on yourself. Report any undesirable conduct. Treat your co-workers and all the people you come across day to day with respect. They are human. The first thing to do when you are stuck in an environment full of drama, back-stabbing, gossip and rumours is to get daily communications happening. Trust and transparency are the antidote to drama. If you witness people engaging in drama do something about it. Don't wait for it to happen a second or third time, call it out. It shouldn't become the norm. Take it off the menu by bringing it to the attention of those involved. A healthy work culture doesn't have space for drama.

48. Never gossip

How it works

When you participate in work place gossip, you need to understand that you can also become the subject of chin-wagging conversations. Therefore, always reflect about what you're saying about others and ask yourself would it be okay if others were talking about you in the same regard. Place yourself in the shoes of anybody being gossiped about. It's really not a nice thing. Gossip can destroy the culture of a company. It can drive people to say and do stupid things. It can lead to people suffering. Imagine for a minute some colleagues having a tongue wag about a colleague who was out the night before and met somebody and maybe went home with them. Imagine these colleagues laughing and talking behind their back, stretching truths and inventing stories with alternative endings of what could have happened. Maybe they are having a laugh, but now imagine that if that person was there and hears everything and starts crying and defending themselves about something that is nobody's business but theirs.

What to do

Gossip can cause disruption to productivity at work. It can cause good people to leave their job. It can create a toxic environment that results in the customers being put second and not first. Some people love to know what's going on in the day-to-day lives of others. Often times, the intention is a conversation starter but it can spiral out of control. Other times, we can give too much information about ourselves to others causing ourselves to be the centre of gossiping. A few simple rules I learned about speaking about people:

- Keep your private life private.
- If you speak about somebody speak as if they are in the room.
- Always address the person by name.
- Be willing to invite the named person into the conversation.
- Speak about others with facts and respect.

If there is gossip about you, face the source. If you feel you can't do this, document factual events and report it. You can also choose to let it go and often times when you don't give it fuel the flame can go out on their own. Lead by example by never participating in gossip.

49. Smile and dial

How it works

The phrase *'smile and dial'* originated in the world of sales. When salespeople cold-called new potential clients they would rhyme off the mantra *'smile and dial'* before each call. Nobody wants to hear a downbeat lazy and insecure voice on the other end of the line. The mantra works equally for customer centre teams. Smiling when speaking changes the sound of the voice to the point where the listener can actually identify that in the tone of your voice. It relaxes the listener. What you are saying is delivered with a more positive manner.

What to do

It's nice to hear a smiley voice answering the phone. It is nice to deal with people who sound happy to help. The smile makes this happen. If you are not a natural smiler start practising. It's a case of fake it until you make it. Practice in front of a mirror. It might feel bizarre but you will see the difference. Your tone will change. You will have an air of enthusiasm in your voice. This creates an immediate picture of somebody who is present. It gives an impression of somebody who wants to listen and wants to help. If you work in an office, put a small mirror on your desk as a reminder. After a while, it will become second nature to you.

If you are having a bad day and can't find the will to smile remember the customer doesn't want to know your problems, they want you to know their problem. They aren't just paying for a product or service. They are paying for your time. Start with a smile. It tends to serve and solve. Smiling affects the way you speak and sit and the way you are received when you deliver a message. If you are having an off day and just can't smile, remember the paying customer does not know and most likely doesn't care how bad your day is going. They can't help you. But you can help them. Your one task is to serve them. If you don't feel good on the inside, get out your smile for the customer. Make the effort. Tone and manner is everything. Smiles are contagious. More smiles mean more sales and more problems solved.

50. Improve response time

How it works

Too many customers all over the world are left hanging on the phone listening to bad music being interrupted by an automated voice recording telling them that they are in a cueing system and that their call is important. Equally, many customers call companies to look for answers to their question to be told that somebody will get back to them and it never happens. The longer it takes to answer a call or solve a problem the more space there is for poor performance in the workplace. People forget to follow-up or they have done their part and the task is sitting on somebody else's table. In cases like these there is normally no follow-up and poor lack of accountably. If you want to improve response time in a call centre or service industry reduce the time and people involved in reaching a conclusion.

What to do

Sometimes when everybody is responsible, nobody is accountable. Ownership of the call, problem or situation needs to be clear. Look at how many people are needed to solve issues or problems that a customer would face. A lot of time can be saved by giving permission to the frontline heroes to make decisions without having to ask permission or get a stamp of approval. It involves training and trust. Once there is clarity on frontline ownership you can turn your attention to measuring your minutes. Reduce your response time or call centre hold-times. Measure productivity. Measure the time when the problem was raised to the moment it was solved and how many people were needed to be involved to solve it. When you do this it's easier to track the timeline and address the bottlenecks. It allows for better communication and follow-up. In 2006, The City Bin Co. sent an internal survey out to all the frontline heroes to ask them about their interactions with customers and the responses. Nigel Disken responded that one of the customer's called the call centre to have his bin emptied. The customer was expecting the service the next day. The bin was emptied within 10 minutes of that call. The customer's response to Nigel was: *'An ambulance wouldn't be as quick'*. This happened because of the call centre's training and follow-up to see was there a truck in the area that could get the job done. Amazing customer service is delivered when expectations are met with a super response. We live in an age where the customers want instant results, next day deliveries and real time follow-up. Don't put off for tomorrow what you can do today.

51. Embrace customer service automation

How it works

Customer service automation is a hotly debated topic that often divides opinions. Some people love the face-to-face interaction. The human connection is unbeatable, or is it? Some are fascinated by technology and the world of AI, contactless payment, other technologies that change and disrupt the current systems that we would have considered normal. Banks are an example of an industry where the human touch has largely disappeared in favour of self-service machines. Instead of walking up to a counter in a bank, you will be either self-serving at a bank machine or doing your banking online or on your phone. McDonalds have gone automated in most of their stores. Now, when you walk into a McDonalds you will approach a touch screen menu where you place and pay for your order. By the time you reach the counter your order will be almost ready to be served to you.

What to do

Automation is not a complex system. Yes, it can be an overwhelming experience to have so many different systems to remember. When designing any part of your business model, make it automated to keep it simple and user friendly. Where you may not be in a position to automate all your business, ask yourself: What part of your business could you automate? Online orders, sign-ups, invoicing, quotes, payments, sales or training. There are many business models which address the idea of automation, however, not all businesses can be automated. Automation when done right needs to create speed and efficiency. For me, I have grown to love it. I do understand the importance of having people at the front line, but where it can improve the customer experience I say embrace it.

52. Get the focus right

How it works

The attitude of your team from top management to the frontline heroes is the difference between convincing lip service and amazing customer service. To set the right tone for your customer you must focus on yourself. When your customer walks into your place of business they know within seconds if you are sincere about helping your customers or your only focus is on the transactional element of the business. If you decide to be a customer focus orientated business, you need to do that so well that transactions will happen because of your service delivery, otherwise you are a sales orientated business. The City Bin Co. never sees itself as a waste company, they have always been a customer focused service company. The offering just happens to be waste collection. In reality, it could be anything else. The focus is always on delivering an amazing service. It drives every conversation, every product and every decision made internally.

Your focus and culture defines every communication between you and your colleagues, between you and your customers and between your customers and their friends and family. In other words, if you create a culture of amazing delivery it will touch every conversation with the focus always on fast delivery, delivering efficiently and delivering with care. Culture is what drives the delivery of amazing customer service. Culture starts with the people. Culture is the environment in which the people work and communicate. When you focus on your internal company culture you will shine a light on your customer service as seen by your customers.

What to do

This is all about placing yourself in the shoes of your customers. First thing to look at is where your focus is. Is everything about sales? Is everything about marketing? Is everything about the transactions? Invite your existing customers to a customer focus group and ask them. Sometimes you believe you have a brilliant customer service ethos and maybe you do but if that does not transcend to the customer's interpretation of what you deliver you have to bridge that gap. The best people in position to tell you possible short comings are your existing customers. When you understand where your focus is as perceived by your customers you can dial into where you need to be and start getting the focus right.

53. Wear a uniform

How it works

I am a big advocate for trying to create a strong corporate image or brand, and to do that a branded uniform can help you stand out in the right places and be miles a head of the competition. You can build on a first impression but you will have it tough to build on a bad impression or where you left no impression at all. An easy win is a smart uniform that stands out and gives you a chance to project a polished and professional image. Uniforms create visibility. The impact of a uniform is both visual and non-visual. On one hand, it is worn to create a visual message and on the other hand it can make you feel part of a team. The uniform helps to set standards by encouraging people to be more aware of their behaviour. They create a first impression giving the company a sense of professionalism and the customers a sense of direction. Uniforms have a big impact in the way customers see your business and how you and your team act while working. When you present a professional image through a common brand that is recognisable you create trust and transparency. Uniforms appear neater and professional. It tells the customer you are skilled and knowledgeable. Uniforms give a sense of team increasing employee pride and morale, which increases productivity and customer satisfaction. A uniform doesn't have to be from head to toe. It could be just a polo shirt with the company colours and logo. Once it is identifiable by the customer and helps the team be more united it's serving its purpose.

What to do

Consult with the staff and empower them to make the decisions on having a uniform and about which choice of uniforms they would like. This is key to ensuring a smooth implementation and positive attitude about the uniform. When you wear a uniform, you create an impression of equality or minimise differences within your team. Sometimes implementing an all-round uniform policy is not necessary. At The City Bin Co. it is just the customer facing employees that wear the uniform. The workers on the trucks and at the bring centres. The sales team are generally dressed in suits, shirt and tie and the office team who have little to no visual contact with customers are dressed smart casual. Think of the fabric, style and service to your business and brand. The most important thing is that you and your colleagues feel comfortable and confident in the uniform.

54. Mind your manners

How it works

Amazing manners are the foundation of delivering amazing customer service. If you want to win business, hit targets and grow your business you have got to mind your manners. Manners are an indication of professionalism and something I see less and less of. This is about practicing thoughtfulness, thinking about how you speak to people and how you address people. It's the thank you, excuse me, and my pleasure that make a difference. Saying thank you goes a long way! It's about being present and not interrupting the flow of conversation. Hold a door for a stranger or offer your seat to another person. Going to a canteen to grab a quick coffee? Offer to get one for your colleagues or customers. Be kind. Think of others. That, to me, is good manners.

What to do

Build a culture of good manners. Start with the basics, *'good morning'*, *'good afternoon'* and *'good evening'*. Address work colleagues and customers by name. Don't pass anybody that is on your team or a customer without giving a warm greeting. If you don't get the basics right, it won't happen. Look at body language. Don't cross arms, or legs and always make eye contact when speaking. Say, *'It's my pleasure'* and thank your customers for their time. Leave the personal social media and private messages for break time or home time. Manners are not an old-fashioned social etiquette taught to you by your parents. They are tools for building lasting relationships in your personal and professional life. Mannered people are responsible people who create opportunities to create and connect with others by being kind. Professional manners get positive attention. Talents and know-how on the job are essential, but if you arrive to work every day with manners you earn respect and possibly even contribute to wowing customers with what can sometimes be missing in business today. Be kind and mind your manners.

Amazing Customer Service
is the new standard for your amazing
Customers

55. Get out the red balloons

How it works

Celebrate your new customers. In 2013, The City Bin Co. was looking to stand out when we delivered our signature red bins to our new customers for the garbage, food and recycling materials. The new customers were already receiving welcome emails which included a *bill of rights* and *a brand promise*. We wanted something a little different that celebrated signing up to the company. Something that would let their neighbours, friends and family know that they were flying with our red bins.

When you think of celebrating, you generally think of a party and parties have balloons. We attached three helium-filled balloons to every new bin delivered. The idea came to life after the marketing team had one of their regular brainstorming sessions to explore how we could make the excellent customer experience even better.

I sourced a supplier of red balloons and helium cylinders. It wasn't an easy task to source five thousand printed balloons and cylinders of helium, with top-ups every other day, but after a broad search, I found Irish Party Supplies. My contact was Bronwyn, who later told me that we were their biggest new customer that year. They learned from us and they were celebrating that. The balloons worked. An idea so simple and different, it was a success. People took to social media to talk about the red bins and the balloons and soon after, new customers were signing up because they saw the red balloons.

What to do

Have a party and get out the red balloons! Firstly look for a way to celebrate the onboarding of every new customer that is visual to them and to others. Make sure that logistics are easy to implement and continually delivered. Consistency is important. If you satisfy a new customer, they will recommend your business. Should they make a purchase, they will expect the same experience. Use the opportunity to send an important message or value. For The City Bin Co., it was our company logo, with the text **We Love Service** printed on each balloon.

Onboarding isn't just about your product or service. Wowing customers is part of the experience. When you celebrate the customer, you are thanking them. Set the standards. Start as you mean to go on. One of my favourite examples of this is from a company called ProsperWorks. They send handwritten notes to each of their new customers that say the following: *'Howdy, Just sending a note to let you know that we love you. Thank you for being a ProsperWorks Customer! You equal Awesome. If you ever need anything, give us a holler. Much love, The ProsperWorks Crew'*.

Some companies make a call or an email. These are useful too but they are not a celebration. You need to find something that says, *'Welcome to the club'* that also lets others know what they are missing.

56. Customer service is the new marketing

How it works

In December 2015, I had the pleasure of an in-depth conversation with Anne Marie Forsyth, the CEO of CCA-Global, a customer contact association that see themselves as the voice of the customer service industry. They identify with what amazing customer service looks like and introduce these standards by working with 1000 plus leading businesses throughout the globe. I was pitching my marketing book to them with the idea to get a speaking engagement. I was excited to speak to Anne Marie and tell her about my bestselling book on sales and the upcoming marketing book I was promoting. Anne Marie listened to my pitch and in one line spoke a simple truth. She said; **'Customer service is the new marketing'**. This line stuck with me. Marketing is too often said to be about creating and promoting the story. Once upon a time the companies would create and fabricate such stories to portray their image in a certain manner, all too often stretching truths. Today, the customers are in control of these stories. In many cases, customers have bigger platforms than the corporate world. Your only job is to make sure you give each and every customer an excellent experience that gives them nothing but a positive and personal story to tell. One example of a platform used by customers to tell their story is *TripAdvisor*.

What to do

Most good hotels and restaurants will invite you to leave a review on *TripAdvisor*. Amazing stories travel fast and not so great stories travel faster. When making a decision to deal with one company or another, a potential customer will research online for reviews and ratings. It's a company's job to read these objectively and response to them with respect. This is the space where you will find your stories and your marketing material. If feedback for your company is largely positive build your marketing around that. If the reviews are not positive, do something about it. Yes, sometimes customers can be fussy or can get it wrong, but they can't be all wrong. The first thing you can do in a case where somebody gives a less than favourable review is to respond, but not just with words. Respond with actions. Fix the problem and invite the customers to try your new updated service. Thank them for pointing out your shortcomings. Where are your customers rating you and are you there to respond?

57. Celebrate your customers

How it works

In August 2012, The City Bin Co. celebrated its fifth year of providing excellent customer service with their waste collection to residents in Dublin by rewarding its first ever Dublin customer with five years' worth of free waste collection. The City Bin Co.'s first ever customer, Louise Purcell was pleasantly surprised when the Managing Director of The City Bin Co. called to the door of her home with a big bouquet of flowers, a specially designed celebration cake, a bottle of champagne and a voucher for five years free waste. For Louise, the visit from The City Bin Co.'s Managing Director was a huge surprise and an amazing treat. For the company, there was a genuine feeling of gratitude to Louise and every single customer that followed. The City Bin Co. celebrate not just our first customers, but many other milestones such as consistently high recycling rates by customers. They let them know that due to their excellent recycling that they are a Top 10% Recycler with a personal note from the CEO. It's the company's way to celebrate the customer and promote positive recycling behaviour. The company also help and celebrate commercial customers who have really good recycling outputs by presenting them with a *'Zero Waste Award'* for having 100 percent recycling success in their business. Some companies celebrate the customer's birthday. To celebrate your customer is to acknowledge the customer's choice to be with you. This can be with a thank you note or a simple phone call that makes a personal connection.

What to do

Firstly, celebrate all your customers. Without them you don't have a business. They are your source of income; therefore, I highly recommend you celebrate every one of them with a personal touch of some sort. If you are lucky enough to have too many customers, start by having a monthly customer appreciation day where you invite them for a coffee and chat. You will learn more about your own product and fix any concerns by simply giving your customers the opportunity to connect with you. Arranging a customer appreciation day is an excuse to celebrate your customers and show them why they are important to you. It can be a big deal with music, party hats and giveaways, or it can be a low-key affair with a select few customers having tea and coffee. Test the waters and see what works for you. When you shine a light on your customers, they will be so surprised and sure to spread the word! It's all about positivity.

58. Map out your customer's journey

How it works

Imagine the only contact you have with your customer is a monthly invoice. That means every time your customer sees your brand they may see it as a negative. A negative because you are taking their hard earned money out of their hand. Yes, you are providing a service or sending a product, but they need more than just the invoice to prove they are paying for an experience. Each time a customer has contact with your brand it is an opportunity to check the connection.

Imagine that your company's point of contact is now more than just invoices. The customer gets news about the product, industry and community through blogs and social media. Maybe you have a company podcast. They will receive welcome letters, updates, personal holiday messages, routine customer calls, newsletters, and service/product satisfaction surveys. Now there are more points of contact to give positive brand engagement. At The City Bin Co., every customer receives a welcome pack, monthly recycling reports, newsletters and regular calls from our customer centre team.

What to do

Check your customer's brand engagement experience by mapping out the customer's journey from start to finish. Think of every point of contact and every possible point of interaction. There are always untapped opportunities. Include all the positive and negative touchpoints. Let everybody in your company see it as they may be able to add more from where they stand within the company and how they interact with the customer.

Ferrari World theme park in Abu Dhabi have their customer journey painted on the wall of their head office in the UAE. Staff and visitors see it every day. Displaying your customer journey like this is a positive way to allow it to be part of the culture. Think of the ways that a customer comes into contact with your brand from the very first moment until you say goodbye. Goodbye is as important as hello. You want to always leave the door open for their return.

Netflix send emails that say, *'We are sorry to say goodbye. Obviously, we'd love to have you back. If you change your mind, simply restart your membership to enjoy!'*

The City Bin Co. have a low churn rate with customers who leave because they are moving to a new house or they are leaving the area. In all cases where a customer chooses to leave the service, we capture the information with an exit interview carried out over the phone by one of our customer centre team.

When you map out your customer's journey and you can see all the touch points, see if there is anything that doesn't need to be there. If you add a new touch point, be sure that it gives value and a positive outcome to the customer.

59. Create customer communities

How it works

When I say create customer communities I am really saying nurture an environment for your already existing customers to communicate freely the good and the bad about your product or service. This is where you will find your super fans. It's also a place where doubts are answered and solutions are found. It's a place a potential customer will go for insights and reviews. It's a place where you will find reviews from poor to excellent. Personally, I prefer to hear about other customer's experiences from another customer as opposed to a sales person or customer centre representative. When I really like something, I will normally go to other users for information, especially when there is a large community. Most brand communities build their community using forums and social media groups. There are also many communities that have strong local chapters and events that bring thousands together around a particular product or brand. Such examples would be the PlayStation community, the Harley Davison biker's groups and Apple users. Your social media pages may serve as a place for your customers to share their thoughts on your product or company. Another important place is your website where you can host a help page answering frequently asked questions.

What to do

Ask your own customers to run and facilitate a user group. Hold customer feedback workshops. Ask them to set up a customer focus group that meet and review your product and make recommendations for improving your product from the standpoint of a non-biased user. Let your existing customers become your source for insights and trusted information for future customers. They have a superior understanding of other customers' requirements and sometimes more so than a customer service representative. When you allow your customers to get involved and contribute to forums, online groups and events you empower them to share their knowledge and experiences by engaging with like-minded people. They create a network. Whether you have a community online or offline it is important that you allow it to grow, respond with respect and engage with the users. Start small. Look for one or two of your existing customers to be your product ambassadors that might champion these platform and events. Give them access to the material they need to begin and grow something especial for the super fans of your service or product. Amazing customer service supporters create brand loyalty.

60. Keep your churn-rate down

How it works

I first heard the word **churn** at a management meeting in The City Bin Co. many years ago. Embarrassed not knowing what it was, I did a quick google search which defined churn as a large metal container for milk. I knew it wasn't that! The second meaning was defined as follows: *Churn is when an existing customer or repeat client stops doing business with your company.* While you have your potential customers that the sales team is trying to bring in the front door, if the service is poor you could be losing existing customers out the back door. The difference between the two is the churn. This is one of the single most important KPIs any company can have on their daily or weekly updates. If this number is rising there is something not right. If your business is a bucket and the water is customers, churn is what happens when you get holes in the bucket. If you don't address the holes in the bucket, the holes get bigger and you are eventually left with no water. Fix the holes by getting the right customers and by fixing the experience. When you fix the holes, you keep your churn rate down. You keep your existing customers.

What to do

There are many ways to calculate your churn rate. If your customers are subscription customers you measure the percentage of customers that have exited your service over a given period. There are two types of customers that fall into this category. The first is the customer who doesn't renew a subscription and the second is the customer that actively cancels before the renewal date. When this happens, you have a very short window to address any issues and successfully ease the termination. This measurement can be daily, weekly, quarterly or yearly depending on the service or product. If you have once off customers or walk-in customers that may not be repeat customers you can measure this by day, week, quarter or against the same period the year before. This allows you to quickly see if you need to refocus marketing efforts. Understanding your churn rate is like taking your pulse rate. You rapidly know if you are in good health. You need to decide what is the churn rate that best measures your success. It is primary a measurement of customer retention; however, it can be applied to other parts of the business. It could be product numbers. It can be applied to profits, staff turn-over, compliments or complaints received in a given phase of your business. Measuring your churn rate truly allows you to know your customers' lifetime value.

61. Measure customer loyalty

How it works

What gets measured gets managed. Every business would like to know their customers' level of loyalty. The great thing about numbers is they do not lie. It's not a story or a grade. It's a simple number that tells you where you are and where you need to be next. At The City Bin Co., we use the Net Promotor Score (NPS). It's a survey conducted by email or phone which asks the customer one simple question: *'How likely are you to recommend our company and service to a friend or colleague?'* The customer rates on a scale of 0-10, and the response is divided up into three categories:

1. **Detractors** are customers who score rate you between 0 – 6. They think little of the service and quality of the product. They would more than likely leave at the drop of a hat for another more attractive offer to save a few pennies.

2. **Passives** are customers that score between 7 – 8. They are very much on the fence. They won't be shouting your praises but at the same time with a little work they can become promotors.

3. **Promoters** are customers that rate you and your company between 9-10. These guys are loyal. They will convert others and they will write positive reviews and tell the world about their experience with you.

To calculate your NPS, detract the percentage of Detractors from the percentage of Promoters. It is that simple. Your score can fall anywhere between -100 and +100. The Global average is +14. At The City Bin Co., we average +73 per month. It's a fantastic method to measure your customers' level of loyalty. It does two things. It tells you if your customers are impressed by your company enough to tell all their friends and family about it and it gauges their satisfaction. It's like being a fly on the wall while your customers are chatting about your product. It allows you to be proactive and not reactive.

What to do

Start by sending out an email to a percentage of your customers. Test the water in terms of what you can handle. It can take a bit of time to manage. When you get a *Detractor*, you may want to investigate further and resolve any issues or gripes. You don't want to become another spam emailer in someone's inbox so I recommend that you think about how you will connect with them and how often will you perform the NPS survey.

You do not need to get permission to use NPS. The process is free. In fact, you have more than likely used it already. Nearly every booking platform and hotel use this method. Last January when I was getting my fiber-optic router installed the cable guy wasn't out the door two minutes when I got a call asking me to rate his visit between one and ten. You can hire companies to manage the process on your behalf or you can do it yourself.

Fred Reichheld who invented NPS once stated: *"One of the most important decisions I made in creating NPS was to make it an open-source movement. As a result, there has been an explosion of creativity from the NPS user community around how the metric and system can be applied."* This means you can be as innovative as you want in applying the procedure to your customer base.

62. Celebrate customer compliments

How it works

At the City Bin Co. there is a flow of gratitude and compliments that arrive as unsolicited written praise from customers on a regular basis. In fact, it would be unfair to refer to these as testimonials, as they say so much more. The City Bin Co. has renamed these tributes, good news stories and compliments as WOWS! One happy customer was so wowed by the service that she was inspired to write a poem about The City Bin Co. They arrive into the call centre or through contact with the employees on the frontline and directly to the CEO. They come in by email, snail mail and direct calls as well as messages left on blogs and social media platforms. Adjacent to the canteen in the Headquarters in Galway, Ireland, there is a huge wall that we know as the 'Wall of WOWs'. This is where we collect customer testimonials. It is a form of celebrating the customer and a daily reminder that reinforces the important message to all that pass it that delivering amazing customer service is at the heart of the company. The WOW's! comprise of a variety of complimentary messages and cover topics ranging from prompt service, going over and above to help a customer, clarity of the communications, kind words for the friendly and well-mannered staff and more.

What to do

You can't fake the sentiments of your customers sending compliments. I have seen competitors try and fail. If the compliments aren't forthcoming, focus on changing the delivery of your service until it's a step ahead of the expectation and industry standard. When you do get positive feedback place it on display. Give it a name, something that suits your personality and the company where you work. It could be your 'Wall of Praise' or 'Feedback files' or 'Positive Vibes'. If you don't have the physical space make it digital. Use a page on your website or a dedicated social media channel. Circulate some of the wows to your team or customers by email or in a newsletter as a means of sharing the customers' appreciation. Focusing on the Wows is a case of success promotes success because when you celebrate the compliments you set the bar and raise product delivery standards. You create a winning mind-set within your company. You see ways to fix the complains and make them compliments. It is a measurement and a mentality. The City Bin Co. have been celebrating customer compliments for over a decade. Start with one and build on that.

63. Always tell customers why you got into business

How it works

When a business starts up, it normally has a 'Why' element to its story. This may be because the founders of the business believed they could offer a better service, or do things so differently that they could disrupt the market. It may be a better way they saw to offer a cheaper product than the current competition. For The City Bin Co., the founders, Gene Browne and Glenn Ward started the company with the view to bringing a new standard of customer service to an industry that was behind the curve when it came to customer values and principles. Today, 23 years on, every single person in The City Bin Co. knows the company's 'Why'. Although the industry has caught up on delivering customer service, our drive to deliver better is still at the front of mind and it is a pleasure to tell our existing customers and new customers why the founders of the company went into the waste management business in the first place. The 'why' you are in business or 'why' the company was founded is often the real reason why your customers fall in love with you in the first place. Too often, that spark needs to be relit.

What to do

Telling your customers why you got into business should happen in some form at every point of the business. At a sales meeting, it needs to be part of the pitch. When standards are not met, you have to put up your hands. You have to reflect on how it should be and the way to look at this is to bring it back to the start. It's an honest and genuine technique that grounds the conversation, especially if things are not going as well as they might with a customer. If a customer calls you up with a complaint, you can tell them exactly why the business was started and ask for another opportunity to demonstrate what is so good about your service. You could say: *'Anne, thank you for sharing your experience with me. When this company was founded it was started on the vision of delivering an amazing service that would be hassle-free. That was not the case this time with you and I would like to offer you another option to validate the real service that we can deliver to you'.* It's a simple communication that reinforces the values of the service, not just to the customer but to the employees delivering the service. It sets the bar for the team and the expectations for the customer going forward.

64. Always get back to the customer

How it works

In January 2018, I had two completely different customer experiences with two separate companies. The first was with my online publishing house, *CreateSpace* which I used to distribute my books to the global online bookstores. I had an issue with the online portal. Their only means of contact was by email. Within two minutes of sending the email with my concern I received an automated email stating that they would reply within twenty-four hours. Sure enough, they replied with a satisfactory resolution within the stated timeframe.

The second experience was when I called my insurance provider only to be put on hold for more than twenty minutes and passed to three different people. All this for a simple change of address, which they promised to send information to me via post to the new address. Sounds familiar? It doesn't end there. After a few weeks, nothing arrived and I called again only to learn that the address was not changed. Back to square one. I asked if they could email the information and they said they would check. They put me on hold and I waited for ten minutes. When the agent returned, she apologised that she forgot about me and we had to start all over again. Eventually, it was resolved. However, this comical scenario is all too common.

It can be tough to have the answers for the customer at the moment they call, but how we handle the call can say a lot to the customer about our service. Keeping a person on hold for a lengthy period and letting the customer know how you will respond and then following up with a closing response can be the difference between a customer who is frustrated with the lack of response and real customer service.

What to do

It can be tough to have all the right answers ready when a you get a call from a customer with a problem or question that needs time to resolve. However, it is your responsibility to follow-up and make the process as easy and calming as possible. Nobody likes to wait when they don't know for how long they will be on hold or if they will get an answer at all. Have a one-call fix. This is the method used at The City Bin Co. When a customer calls they can have a peace of mind that when they hang up the job is done. The agent is responsible for dealing with the request. Decide on a channel of communication that will be best for communication with the customers. Measure how many queries there are and how long it takes to respond and resolve them. When analysing the types of queries, you should focus on reducing of time taken to action solutions for them. Always look for long-term solutions and not a quick fix.

65. Use technology to provide a better service to your customers

How it works

I am amazed how differently I do my tasks today compared to ten years ago. I continue to do most of the same jobs, however many of the methods I would have used are now redundant. I have gone from working a high percentage of my time on the laptop to nearly one hundred percent on my mobile phone. I have gone from office based to more remote work. I don't have to go to the office to log into my salesforce jobs. I go straight to the application on my phone. Yes, these applications were around ten years ago. The difference is they are faster and simplified. Ten years ago, I was in front of my computer every morning planning my day and answering emails. Now, I am at my first meeting virtually, or in person. So, how do you bring your business into a technology driven world where your customers are now comfortably spending their time? You don't have to reinvent the wheel. There is a system or application solution with everything from delivery applications to simple invoicing tools, chat-bots and advanced calendar organisation systems.

What to do

Look at what can help you to save time, space or money and provide a better service to your customer. Start with your websites. Provide a page where you can answer questions for your customers and allow them to get answers from other customers. Cut your communication cost by using social media as a tool to support your customers. Look at all the software you are using and investigate if there are alternatives available. Often, we stick to the same CRMs because they are 'just there'. Now, look at the tasks you do that don't have a significant technology behind them and research if there is a application out there that can do the job. Ask, what do you do manually and is there something available to move the process faster, better and maybe cheaper. Enable your frontline staff to use a smartphone or tablet to stay connected with their team and communicate 'on the go'. Use a project management tool or calendar system such as Teamup, Trello, or Doist. Do you have a server room? Yes, it may have cost you a lot to install 10 or 20 years ago but time to consider the cloud now. The main thing to do is an audit of every task you do today and investigate if there is a technology that will allow you to give a better service to others.

66. Create case studies

How it works

There are two types of cases studies that can be used for the benefit of providing amazing customer service. Firstly, a case study where you highlight successes between you and your customers. Success can come from complaints or compliments. The idea is to document the case in a factual manner so that other colleagues can benefit from your experience. This results in better customer experiences and more confident workers. You are using the tool for internal learning that brings an educational value helping explain different cases within your company. When these are done continuously over time you will begin to create a library of references and situational clarifications for cross learning that allows for a companywide learning pool. It helps all the teams to be equipped with the maximum knowledge to tackle any situation. A second use for the case studies is as an external sales and marketing tool to showcase your current and past achievements with certain aspects of your product. At The City Bin Co. we created many case studies around our success in helping our clients increase their recycling rates. When we presented this to another customer it showed them the path. It demonstrated that it was possible.

What to do

When creating case studies, firstly, decide what purpose you want them to serve. Will they be created to help your team or will they be created to show the customer something that you feel will enhance their experience. Keep them short. Give them a name that resonates with your business. Include a picture. State the situation. Where it took place. What steps you took in approaching the situation. Who was involved. When it took place and the preventative measures taken so it won't happen again or if it does happen everybody will know the best response. If the case studies are only for internal use, be sure to mark it so. If the case study is for presenting to customers, get it proof read and make sure it is professionally presented. The case studies can also be an add-on to share with visitors to your website.

67. Set the tone

How it works

When you are communicating to your customer by email, in person or on the phone, the tone you use is key in delivering a credible customer focused approach. Tone isn't just the friendly manner in which you speak to customers. That's just one element. Tone includes your greetings, your time with the client and the undivided attention you give. Tone includes the way you carry yourself; Are you in uniform, well-dressed or do you look like something the cat dragged out of bed. Tone is your engagement. Are you willing to solve, or do you pass the buck? Tone is your energy. Are you focused and attentive or are you giving more attention to your phone or emails then the customer on front of you. Tone is the consistent yet flexible interactions between your brand and others.

What to do

To set the right tone you have to think about your audience. Who are they and how do they resonate with you. How do they speak and how do you speak with them? Develop your voice. Communicate with the values and words that represent your company to connect with the customer. Communication should always flow. Always be relaxed, so your communication comes naturally. Never start with the issues, start with the greetings. Think about the best way to greet customers. You need to cautiously choose your words to avoid awkwardness or vagueness. Brief, carefully worded sentences help keep your message clear and avoid misinterpretation. You have to be yourself enough to convey sincerity but confident enough to express the message of your company. The tone of expression needs to demonstrate your personality and also the values of your brand through coherent communication that resonates with customers and builds trust through familiarity. The best way to hone your tone is to allow for feedback. This can be done between colleagues or by asking the customers after an interaction. When you receive feedback you can enrich your overall delivery. If you have an excellent tone, your interactions should seem easy and positive no matter what the challenge or problem. The end goal of an amazing tone is to enhance the experience that the customer has with you and that they feel good about the communication.

68. Speak your customer's language

How it works

When I speak about the customer's language, I'm not talking about mirroring their words or speaking Spanish, French or English. I'm talking about customer experiences. It's about their experience. You and what you represent is part of that experience and that's the secret to speaking their language. Give them an experience they'll love and listen to them. To speak your customer's language, you must tune into their needs and communicate your offer or solution in a way that they understand.

The best way to do this is to allow them to be comfortable in your space and in control of their decisions. **Tell, don't sell.** The most important aspect of speaking your customer's language isn't just the verbal communication, but your ability to make your customers feel relaxed, appreciated and in control.

What to do

Ask for feedback. Learn from each interaction how to better serve your ideal customer. Don't pressure your customers to give certain answers. Instead, take note of what they think of your service. Learn who your customers are and what they need by listening, understanding and revising the points of contacts with your customers. Their needs are not only about the product they're looking for but the experience. Listen to each customer and ask if they require assistance. Maybe they need time to browse. Do they understand your product? Do they want to come back? If you want them to care you have to care.

Speaking the customer's language shouldn't be an effort. It's a process of getting to know your customers so well that they feel good when buying from you. Make them want to come back again and again for the experience. Look at every point of contact that your customer has with your business, not only that the business has with the customer. Look at different points of contact the customer may have outside the business. Maybe there's a bus stop outside the business, maybe it's a newsletters they've signed up for. If the business operates a delivery service, the vehicle is the point of contact. Sponsorship of local raffles and events also increases visibility.

69. Speak many languages

How it works

While most businesses highlight the importance of the customer experience to their company, their non-English speaking patrons often go unnoticed. A report by the International Customer Management Institute (ICMI) in 2014 found that 86% of contact centres reported having non-native speaking customers.

I love when I fly home from Dubai to Ireland on an Emirates Airlines flight. The pilot always introduces his cabin crew on board and how many languages they speak. Each of the staff wears a little flag that identifies where they are from. I love it when I see some of their Irish staff so I can practise a bit of my rusty Irish or if I see staff with a Spanish flag I practice my Spanish. Emirates Airlines use this little trick to stand out from their competitors. Most airlines have a lot of different nationalities working for them but they don't tune in and take advantage of this in the same way as Emirates Airlines.

In the same way, I remember going into the Home Store on the second floor of the Mall of the Emirates in Dubai and being greeted by a big sign that said '*Welcome. Here we speak many languages*'. 'Welcome' was written colourfully in all the different languages. What Emirates Airlines and the Home Store at the Mall figured out and use so well to build an amazing customer ethos is; as *Paddi Lund, international business author,* coined so well, the *Critical Non-Essentials*. It's the small things that make the difference. In today's internationalised and multicultural world, it is important to know where your customers come from and what languages they are comfortable speaking.

What to do

Identify people within your company who speak different languages fluently and let your customers know how many different languages are spoken in your company. If there is very little, or only one language, create guidelines for using clear and simple language easily understood by non-native speakers. Do a buyer persona project to help identify your current customers and the languages spoken in your target market. Evaluate the scope of customer enquiries. How many calls are from Polish people? How many are from Spanish people? Because of the international population in Dubai, when you call most businesses you will be given the option to speak to somebody in Arabic, English, French or Hindi.

I remember being in The City Bin Co. office in Galway, Ireland, in June 2015 when a customer phoned the customer centre and was struggling to express herself as she had very little English. At the time, we had 13 different languages available in the office. Kate spoke Polish and Russian and Helen spoke French and Niamh was fluent in Irish. I'm fluent in Spanish. The Customer Centre manager, Helen Gately, took the call. She recognised that the customer was struggling to say what she wanted to say. Helen quickly identified that the customer was from Spain. Within seconds, Helen transferred the call to me and I was able to help the customer. Most clients would not expect you to offer support in multiple languages. Firstly, let your staff know what languages their colleagues speak. And secondly to avoid unnecessary disappointment be proactive in updating this information with your clients.

70. Be a super customer

How it works

Too many times we take customers for granted. We don't smile. We are short with them. We let the stresses of our own personal life come into our work life. If you want super customers you need to walk in their shoes and relate to their mind-set and expectations. Nobody should part with their hard-earned cash to be served by somebody who has their mind somewhere else. Just before Christmas, I bought two different books in two different bookshops. The different experiences were like day is to night. In the first shop, the cashier gave me his full attention, made eye contact and spoke with a smile. He asked if I needed anything else before popping the book in a paper bag and thanking me. In the second shop there was no greeting, just a non-engaging request for the price of the book. The cashier was already taking the books from the next person while handing me the change. I said 'thank you', however it fell on deaf ears. From these two experiences I noted the difference for me and how I reacted and I now make sure when I am speaking to my own customers that I greet them in a mannerly fashion and focus only on them. If I move too quickly onto the next customer it takes the approachability and responsiveness out of the contact with clients.

What to do

Many people peep into this space with the eyes of a mystery shopper. I believe that best way to have super customers is to be a super customer. This means being very conscious with every experience you have when buying from others. This may be when you refill your car with fuel or do your weekly shopping. The idea is not to be a critic of others but to be an observer. Ask yourself, how could it have been done better? Was there a smile or eye contact missing? Was there a lack of hygiene with the personal? Was there a sense of friendliness and honesty? Did the interaction leave a positive lasting experience and, if so, what was the secret sauce that left such a good impression with you? Where you do see small details that impress you, take note and apply them in you own way of delivering amazing service. What good points can you take from another industry and apply to yours? For me, it's to be kind and be a super host to your super customers.

71. Recommend your competitors

How it works

When should you send your clients or potential customers to your competitors? When there is no fit between what you offer and their needs. Why should you do it? It shows you are confident in your business, product knowledge and market mindfulness. It demonstrates that you truly put the customers first. When you give an alternative recommendation to a client that you really can't help, it allows you to focus on core clients that you can help. It allows you to give better customer service.

While working in Abu Dhabi in June 2017 an existing client called to enquire if the company would do some roof and window cleaning. This wasn't an unusual request, as some companies like to bundle cleaning and waste services together. What was unusual to my client was that I declined the job and I recommended a competitor. When he asked why I recommended a competitor, I told him it was not a service that we provided and it was the right thing to do. It was good customer service.

As we discussed his needs I realised that we could not provide that particular service. We could have subcontracted it, however, we would have never been able to stand over the quality of work. I was happy to recommend one of my competitors. The client was surprised that I was willing to turn business over to a rival company.

Another time, I was driving back from Abu Dhabi to Dubai after a very long day of work with my colleague James Kent late one evening. We both were very tired and James had a bit of preparation work to do later that evening. We had a small problem. The charger for James' HP Spectre laptop wasn't working. James needed to sort it fast as he had a big sales presentation for a potential client the following morning. I drove James to Sharaf DG, one of the biggest computer stores in the UAE. Ajesh, a representative at the store, greeted us. They didn't have the charger in stock but could order it for the next day. He could not give us an exact time because it depended on the orders and deliveries booked on that day. Ajesh recommended the Computer Plaza in Bur Dubai where we could pick up the charger. That is customer service. Within one hour, James had his charger and the next morning he delivered a killer presentation.

What to do

Customers have long-term memories and you must create an environment where they will remember you for being friendly and helpful. That is why they return. Customers don't buy products or services. They buy experiences. This is a long-term way of thinking that will portray your business as an honest and transparent company. Put your customer's needs before your own. It's that simple.

If you can't provide a product or service but your competitor can, let the client know. Even if they have competing products have the confidence to help the customer and point them in the right direction. Then they will return when they need a service you provide. Why? Because trust has already been build. It works both ways. That person is more likely to recommend your business to others because you have demonstrated professionalism and amazing customer service. The connection has already been made. Think of it as a long-term relationship that cements business with the client or, if not, invites the customer to return in the future should they require your services. The key is knowing exactly what you sell and what you don't.

72. Learn why your customers leave

How it works

You can say to yourself *'You win some, you lose some'* and hope for the best or you can learn why some customers don't return or cancel the relationship with your business by figuring out why they leave and, where possible, do everything to make the customers want to stay because you are simply amazing at what you do. To really win the customers, you have to get amazing at your product delivery and communicate with them on each and every point of contact, even when they decide to leave.

What to do

Identify your service weakness and improve. Instead of promising more than you can give, give more than you promise. Be clear in your offering and consistent in your delivery. Wow your customers every time with a fast follow-up. Give them a positive experience. Always be available to your customers at the time that they need you to be there for them. The Internet has allowed companies to have a 24-hour connection with their customers. Consistency and availability are fundamental. Make sure your customers know when you are available. Be involved in the same social media channels as your customers. Cultivate solutions that reach your individual customers' precise needs. When they say it's time to part ways, find out why by asking them. It's really that simple. Create an exit survey to share with them. There are 4 main reasons why somebody leaves or stops using a service:

- They move out of the geographical location where your product or service is available.
- Their economic situation has changed and they can't afford it or it's not critically essential to their needs.
- They are lured away by a competitor with a better offer.
- They are disappointed by poor product delivery, poor attitude and lack of follow-up.

The first two reasons are out of your hands, however they only account for a small percentage of customers that will cut the cord. I believe that if you focus on fixing the latter two you will keep most of your customers and have an impressive churn rate. This can be done by simply building strong one to one relationships with your customers. Make it easy to do business with you. Be very approachable and contactable. Resolve problems fast. Connect regularly and ask questions to encourage positive dialogue. The goal for your relationship with the customer is that if they are tempted to change to a competitor they will be comfortable to come to you first because you have invested in building a strong relationship with them.

73. Don't let business go down the loo!

How it works

On a trip up the East coast of Spain by train early this year I came across an interesting company called '2theLoo' at Joaquin Sorolla train station in Valencia. They are a company who manage and run public toilets. Their goal is to provide the ultimate public toilet break in an extraordinary way. Their focus is customer service. They took the most unsexy and unloved part of the travel and shopping journey; the loo and turned it into a brilliant business and an amazing experience for customers.

What really wowed me at '2theLoo' was that they changed the view of the poor public toilet where you arrive to find no loo paper, no door, bad smell, uncleaned and explicit graffiti, which was my experience several times over at the bus station in Benidorm over the past three years to one of a positive and clean place to go. 2theloo make the difference by having an onsite friendly and uniformed attendant. They have spacious cubicles cleaned after each use. They have paper and soap supplies always stocked up and free wifi! The rest rooms are a 'pay for use' service where the tickets can be redeemed for local businesses and provide the surrounding businesses with a positive image creating more footfall and better business. The first 2theloo opened its toilet doors in 2011 in the Kalverstraat, Amsterdam showing an impressive growth which have seen 220 locations in 12 countries including Amsterdam, Paris, Madrid, London and Barcelona. Their brand promise; to offer the ultimate public toilet break experience!

What to do

Treat your customer like royalty. 2theLoo took a neglected part of the travel and shopping experience and made it excellent! They turned it into a profitable business. They made the toilet experience better than at home for all their visitors. Look at the neglected part of your business in your shop or premises or online. Look at the experience from the customers point of view. Approach your business with a playful and entrepreneurial mind-set. The neglected part of your business could be your online portal, your payment options or your social media. It maybe the loo! Don't let business go down the loo! A part of your business that you might think is not of interest or not your responsibly may be an opportunity for you to provide an amazing customer service.

Amazing
Customer Service
Happens When You
Turn the Complaints into
Compliments

74. Accept every scenario

How it works

In May 2018, I was returning from a conference when my flight from Gatwick, London in the UK to Alicante, Spain, was delayed. This little setback meant I was to miss my bus from Alicante to Javea, a small costal town about one hour north of the airport. The problem was because I was arriving at 2am at night there was no bus service until the next morning. I was thinking at the time to get a taxi which would work out at 160 euros, at which point it would be cheaper to stay in a local hotel and catch a bus in the morning. As luck would have it, when I exited the terminal I spotted a local bus company called *Benniconnect*, which services the Costa del Sol from and to Alicante airport. I asked the driver if there were any spare seats and there was one! I felt so lucky! The driver's last stop was a small town called Benissa. That was until I came along. Javea was another 20 minutes on top of his already delayed journey and as he was the last of the evening he would have to go to the depot and park up the bus. On arriving to Javea the driver started to ask me about where I was staying. My accommodation was about 10 minutes walk from the bus stop. The driver offered to take me to the front door of my apartment. He was helpful with my suitcases, carrying one of them to the door. As I travel frequently, I now use this service for all of my journeys. Although they don't drop me to the door, I find that the culture of kindness is a theme found in all their employees. The driver that night did not complain. He owned the moment and bent the rules a little to deliver me home safely.

What to do

Accept every scenario. That's what the bus driver did. He accepted the delays. He offered to see me home safe in the middle of the night. He helped with my belongings. **Accept every situation without exception.** When you accept a situation, you don't fight it. You don't complain and you get through it happier and faster. **Approach it with enthusiasm.** When you tackle the gloomiest of tasks with a smile, it's a lot easier to deal with. **Make all customers feel comfortable and safe.** The driver understood that after a long plane and bus journey married with delays I just wanted to get home. He didn't have to, but he helped make this comfortable. He understood I wasn't just taking a bus, but that I was going home. **Think of others. Be of service, not selfish.** The driver's only job was to bring me to the station. He went the extra mile in all senses of the word. And I am deeply appreciative that he did so.

75. If there is a problem, own it and fix it

How it works

You may have an amazing product, but if something happens in the delivery that is out of your hands and it is important, you have to take responsibility and get it sorted. We often talk about customer service when things are going as they should, but real customer service can be seen when something does not go as planned. I was so happy after designing my business cards on Canva.com. I decided to use their service to print them. Within five working days, the cards arrived. I was very impressed with the packaging. It was solid. Inside a strong box was a small white box with the Canva.com logo on top. The packaging was so good it felt like I was unwrapping an iPhone. Inside the box was a small thank you card and a note from the CEO and Co-Founder Melanie Perkins. There was also a gift of some greeting cards, which came in handy as the package arrived on Mother's Day. This was not new for me. I had previously used their services and as before, I was impressed with the effort and thought put into both the product and the delivery of the product. But this time, the product had a slight defect. The business cards were unevenly cut and had paper shavings still hanging off them. It was as if the machine blades for cutting the cards were damaged. As this was not the service I was used to from the company I immediately contacted them via their online Twitter account. Their reply was within 20 minutes and they sent new cards to me within three days. They followed up with an email apologising for the error and provided a timeline of when my new cards would arrive. I was happy with the end result and continue to use them and recommend them.

What to do

Take responsibility to address situations when they arise. Take an ambulance approach to getting to the problem and resolving it as fast as possible. If there is a problem, own it and fix it. Canva.com kept the customer in the loop on their progress. Don't assume your customer will not mind. When you fix something for a customer, take care of them so they will return. If you don't they will go elsewhere. In many cases, there may be a problem but the customer doesn't know how to get in touch. Be contactable across all channels. I chose to contact Canva on Twitter because it was open on my browser at the time.

76. Fix the source of the complaint

How it works

Too often in business the front-line heroes are tasked with fixing the same complaints over and over again. The fact of the matter is that they fix the same problem so often they make it look like there is no problem. The correct action would be to fix the problem at a source level so it never happens again. Instead of fixing the complaint in that moment imagine if the task was to resolve the cause so it never happens again eliminating that complaint from ever happening in the future. This is harder than it appears as it can mean investigating problems at a deeper level that can involve changes of departments, culture and policies. If you can identify a change that can happen that will address the source of a complaint as opposed to just a temporary solution, then do just that.

What to do

Fixing the real source of complaints happens with the training and empowerment of the customer facing staff, the front-line heroes. Often this can be about changing the culture within the company. Firstly, start documenting all complaints that you receive about your product and service, small and large. Looking at this list, categorise which complaints you would like not to have ever repeated again and what changes have to happen to make this happen. Of course, you would want all the complaints to never repeat themselves. Start with 3 on the list and focus on what needs to change to take them off the list. What current process or system is stopping this from happening. Is it a training issue the needs attention? How often are you and your colleagues trained and retrained in the business where you work. Is the training sufficient. Is it once off or repeated? Often times, companies train staff with induction training when they are starting off but never up skill or upgrade the skillset needed to implement the skills needed to cause change. Empower all front-line heroes to implement changes. Reward staff that identify changes that can be made to kill repeat complains from clients.

77. Log and learn from customer complaints

How it works

Often, when things go wrong we get a golden opportunity to let amazing customer service shine. It can be hard to see a complaint as a positive in the moment when it can cause loss of time and money in the short term. However, when we get a solution you can increase customer loyalty turning unhappy customers into happy ones. Complaints that are resolved through your social media channels are witnessed by a wider audience who can produce good stories about your service. All complaints can be solved in the short term but unless they are logged and improvements are made so the same complaints don't happen again, you will not improve your service to customers. When you document the complaints, you create a database and a learning tool of how to resolve issues turning the negative problems to positive solutions.

What to do

The most important action you can take when you receive a customer complaint is to listen, to understand the situation and offer a solution. You could leave it at that but an amazing next step is to log the complaint in a factual format that allows for assessment and improvement. Create a customer complaint log as a simple record to file complaints in an orderly fashion. The file should act as an educational tool that allows you to spot faults within your product and service delivery and change them. Once these changes are made they act as case studies that help employees deal with similar complaints. Many CRMs include systems that allow the user to log complaints or cases. If you don't have these you can create your own simple log. Make sure all cases to log complaints include the following:

1. Date of the complaint
2. Description of the complaint
3. Person responsible for closing out the complaint
4. The solution
5. What needs to change for this complaint not to happen again

Always review your complaint files regularly to see what patterns come up and what long term solutions can happen to prevent a repeat of the same issues and problems. No business is perfect and not every customer will be happy but you can prevent the same old complaints from popping up again and again.

78. It's okay to say no

How it works

It can be very easy to say 'Yes' when a customer is asking for a reduction in price or requesting a service to be done differently. It can be a good thing to go 'off the menu' from time to time to deliver excellent service but, too often, we don't look at the effect on the business in terms of price and time. The fear of losing the business or disappointing the customer can lead to you saying yes to demands which can have a short term positive effect on the customer and a long term negative effect on the business. This is not about limitations, but about defining and knowing the boundaries of the sandbox where you operate. In my mind, saying no to a customer can be a potentially positive action.

What to do

It's okay to say no. What's not okay is if you don't know when to say 'No' or why you are saying 'No' to a customer. Respond as quickly as you can and be honest. Manage customer expectations by being truthful. Learn your service boundaries that tell you when to say no and why you have to say no. Create some simple clarity charts around expectations from the company and anticipations from your customer. This allows you to keep support consistent and manage the customer's expectations. Clear procedures that are communicated to your customer before any service or product is delivered are a powerful way to address this. At the City Bin Co. every new customer on-boarding gets a one page *'Bill of Rights'*. This tells new customers what they can expect from the company and what the company expects from them. Sometimes, customers can not be clear or speak with a lot of emotion and misunderstandings can happen. Never say yes or no right away. Clarify all requests that you are not sure of by asking the customer to explain. You could say *'I am not quite sure I understand what you mean, could you clarify?'* Or you could repeat back the request simply by saying; *'If I understand you correctly you wish to do X and Y'*. Be sure to be compassionate when saying *'No'*. This is done by listening and saying that you understand or straight out saying; *'Please accept my apology'* where possible. Most times, a *'No'* is simply what you can't deliver, so always remember to express your *'Yes'* and assert your *'No'*. The customer may not be happy with your answer, however there is a certain element of damage control and empathy when saying to a customer that you can't be of service. Let it be a positive *'No'* by offering an alternative service, product or even a competitor.

79. Own the call

How it works

Ideally, if a customer wants one or several things done, they should only have to speak with one professional and knowledgeable person to get their answers. Your job is to get the job done right, first time, every time. You should aim to address the customer's need the first time they call, therefore eliminate the need for the customer to follow-up with a second call. To get a one call fix requires detailed understanding of the product. Many call centres and businesses use a metric to measure this called *First Call Resolution* (FCR). This is the measurement of the success of resolving a customer's call on the first contact. The idea is pretty simple in theory but a tough one in practice. The goal is to get to the end of the first call with no follow-up required. This is a high bar to set, although sometimes not possible to reach depending on the complexity of the call. It puts the focus on a high-quality delivery of product and services while keeping cost down. This is about ownership of the call and responsibility for the resolve.

What to do

When a one call fix is not possible as you might have to get help on something with another department make the follow-up commitment to come back within a short time period with a solution. You could say to the caller;

'John, in order for me to get the best result for you I will talk to our operations team. My commitment to you is that I personally will call you back on the number you have provided with a clarification to your questions. I will call within one hour. Is that good for you?'

Always give a commitment of a time and make sure that only you and nobody else calls back. If the caller has to speak to somebody else they will have to start from scratch again and will be back at square one. You need to bring them forward. If it's something you cannot solve, the closest thing to a one call fix is to tell the customer that you will take care of them and do so. Maybe you will have to talk to five of your colleagues in the background to get things done. That's perfectly okay, but own the call until the case is closed.

80. Stick to the facts, not the fiction

How it works

Facts are important when it comes to marketing and sales. You will never have a good business if you invent a story or try to fool potential clients by misleading them. When speaking to disgruntled clients, you must provide facts. But remember that a client will believe that they are right.

Doris Lessing, an Iranian-born British Novelist who won a Nobel Prize for Literature in 2007, wrote in her autobiography, *Walking in the Shade, 'What's true for you isn't necessarily true for me'*. With this quote in mind, that is exactly why we must always get the facts and not the fiction when it comes to communicating with the customer. Understand that what the customer thinks is true for them. Unfortunately, it may not be maintained by the facts. Recognise that they will hold on to this truth. The only way to resolve this is to listen. Do not fight to change their mind.

I remember a customer who called to say his bins were not collected and he saw the truck leaving the area. He demanded to phone the driver immediately and return at once. After he told me what happened, I repeated what he told me. Meanwhile, I was gathering information from the live tracking system. I told him that they were collected and asked him to check the bin. The bin was empty. He couldn't believe it. One of the little things that The City Bin Co. do is, they put the bin back exactly where it was left. The customer said, *'Wow!'* and *'Thank you'*.

What to do

Firstly, listen to their truth. Then repeat it back to them so they can hear their truth. You are not saying you agree. You are empathising with them. You can say, *'Let me summarise what you are saying'*. Understand it from their point of view. Then explain the facts as you see them. Inform them that you will provide a satisfactory solution. By listening and repeating back you will relax them. You are on their side. It is important to listen. If you don't listen, somebody else will and that's when their story goes to friends and on social media. Your business reputation is only as good as your customer's last experience. Everyone on your team that interacts with your customers should understand this.

81. Repeat what you just heard

How it works

If you want repeat customers, start repeating what the customers say to you. Now, I am not saying to start sounding like a parrot. This is really an exercise that confirms the order, query, grumble or question. When I sit down at one of my favourite places, 'the Sheeben' Irish bar in Javea, Spain to have a coffee and snack I am always impressed with the fact that the staff taking the order will repeat back my order. This is common practice in the food and restaurant business and is a simple and wonderful habit to apply to all industries where there is any customer exchange. In fact, repetition is useful in any conversational situation such as problem solving, sales or negotiation where by a conclusion is required by both the customer and the company representative.

What to do

Repeating what someone said back to them needs to be done as paraphrasing. Not parroting. It is a way to look for more detail.

If someone says; *'I had a horrible experience with your service'*. I might ask, *'What was horrible about the service?'*

Or, if a customer calls you to tell you their loyalty card has been stolen you could say; *'I'm really sorry to hear that you have lost your card, tell me more...'*

If you practice this you will become a more attentive listener and will tighten the possibility of error to a minimum. If you want to be excellent at making conversation & delivering solutions you have to be a good active listener. One way to do this is to guide the conversation with inviting phrases such as, *'Yes, tell me more?'* or *'Is there anything else?'* or *'What should happen now?'* Once the customer is finished speaking, summarise what was said by repeating the bullet points of the conversation. This gives the customer a chance to confirm their content. You've got to be slightly savvy when repeating but it's surprisingly effective as it shows that you are listening, interested and responsive.

82. Don't react, reply

How it works

When we react to problems or complaints we are approaching situations emotionally. You need to learn to put your emotions aside. When you put your emotions aside you will respond with respect. Putting your emotions aside doesn't mean that you are not interested or passionate about what you do or who you are speaking to. From time to time, you may have to deal with difficult customers. These customers may be rude, emotionally upset and angry. It can be very hard when you are on the receiving end of such conversations to keep it together. Whether it's a pleasant person simply letting you know what you should do or an irritated customer with no control on their anger, the only way to manage such interactions is by being calm and in control. Easier said than done and the only way to master this is to practice day in and day out.

What to do

Remember nobody goes to work to end up in tears because of what a rude customer said. It is never personal, but we are human and it takes lots of mindfulness and practice to deal with the disgruntled punter. Approach every call with the only intention to be helpful. Yes, it is true that some people don't want an immediate solution and only want to vent. In this case the only thing you need to do is let them vent and listen without getting attached to the emotion driving the conversation. Show empathy by listening and knowing that you don't have to be emotionally attached to the situation. When you invest emotions into the conversation, it is very easy to lose control and end up with the wrong outcome. To keep control, bring your best manners to the forefront. Focus all your attention on the person with whom you are speaking to. Do this by giving them the space to say what they need to say. Thank them for contacting you and sharing their complaint. Summarise their complaint and repeat it back to them. This shows that you are listening. Show empathy by replying in a simple loving manner. **Kill them with kindness** is a phrase that comes to mind. Keep the tone of your voice calm and speak slowly but firmly. Don't react, reply.

83. Deal with angry customers with respect

How it works

In all businesses, you can find a small percentage of customers can be obnoxious, intolerant, belligerent, unpleasant and impatient. Your job is to listen to the other side with the intention of resolving the matter on hand. Imagine that you answer the customer's call, or a customer has suddenly arrived in person at your office. Now imagine, you find yourself on the front line of a whole lot of anger delivered with a deplorable impoliteness. Imagine how you would react? When I worked in both Ireland and Dubai I worked at offices with open plans. I remember on so many occasions admiring the customer centre team when I overheard them speaking to disgruntled customers on the phone. They would display a sense of calmness, brilliant listening abilities, positive response and resolution no matter the difficultly of call with the customer. The way to do this is practice and training. There is an NLP principle that states; **The consequence of your communication is the response that you get.** If you adapt your communication with this in mind, you will, over time, develop the necessary communication skills to bring all of those calls to a satisfactory and timely solution for all parties. You deal with angry customers with respect and learn to request respect from them.

What to do

Always stay calm and don't react to the call emotionally. If the customer is angry and may have a real reason to be so, always remember it is their anger, not yours. The first thing to do is to remain calm and not respond in kind. Don't take it personally. Listen and let them explain their side of the story. Although angry customers may take their frustration out on you, they know that you did not cause their problem. Never argue back. Just listen and, where appropriate, say sorry on behalf of the company. Be patient and give them time to vent. It the product or service failed it is your job to understand what happened and offer a solution. Ask questions to collect facts on the difficulty that the customer has called about. Work with your customer to find an end result that pleases you both. The solution should be reasonable and justified for all involved. Learn how to release any stress caused by angry callers. This is important so any tension isn't brought on to the next call. Take a quick minute to do some deep breathing exercises or have a quick coffee.

84. How to terminate a call with a disgruntled customer

How it works

There is a big difference between a customer being angry and venting their anger with the view of getting a resolution and somebody who is being rude. I would love to say never hang up on a customer but it simply is not true. There are exceptions when callers are over stepping a line and being abusive, intimidating, getting very personal and using vulgar language. When this happens, I believe you have a right to cut the call and that there is a right way to do so. But before doing so, understand that an upset customer has a right to be upset. One should never mistake the justified anger with a lack of sensitivity. You need to utilise empathy in an effort to bring an effective resolution. If this is not possible and the caller is crossing the line you can terminate the call once you have a structure in place that allows you an understanding of what is and is not acceptable from a caller.

What to do

Never just hang up on any customer. That's bad manners! Just because they have crossed a line doesn't mean you have to do the same thing. If you are going to terminate a call you need to give three things: An explanation, a warning and a guarantee to follow-up.

An explanation sets boundaries by explaining to the customer if they continue to speak with bad language or a raised voice you will terminate the conversation and reschedule a call for a later time that same day. Never set boundaries you aren't prepared for nor able to enforce. If you don't follow through, you can lose the control of the call and credibility with the caller.

A warning is given when the customer ignores the explanation and continues with the same manner of speaking. Some companies operate a '3 strikes and the call is discontinued' directive. In giving a warning, you take control of the call and encourage the person to stop the bad conduct so you can help them. At all times use a calm and confident tone of voice.

A guarantee to follow-up is always given before terminating the call and saying goodbye. This needs to be also followed up by email and a call at a later time in the same day. When a call is discontinued by you it is important to follow-up by email and then phone at a later time to close off any remaining issues.

At the end of the day, terminating a call is not a solution; it's a time out. Terminating any call should be a last port of action and should only be done with caution. You may not be able to get a word into get a resolve because of a verbal thunder storm coming down the line. In any case, always be polite and thank the person for their call. Tell them you will be in touch by email, hang up the phone and follow-up.

85. Tune into the tone

How it works

Setting your own tone is one thing. Tuning into the tone of others is more of a listening and observing exercise. According to Dr. Albert Mehrabian, author of *Silent Messages,* after conducting several studies on non-verbal communication he found that 7% of any message is conveyed through words, 38% through certain vocal elements, and 55% through non-verbal elements such as facial expressions, gestures and posture. These are all forms of the tone expressed in communication. The tone is the frequency that you deliver your message. It applies to how you speak, the volume of your voice when you speak, the friendliness, the body language and the willingness to connect. Tone can be negative and positive. You are aiming for the latter. Tone can come across in conversations on the phone or in person. It can be picked up in written communication such as text or email. It can be seen in body language from eye connection to good posture.

What to do

Customers don't normally remember everything that was said during a conversation but what they will remember is the tone of the conversation and how they felt because of the tone. Focus on 3 elements. Your voice, your words and your non-verbal body language. The tone of **your voice** can mean a few different things, but it usually comes down to the emotions expressed by the words you are using. When you are speaking, talk as if your grandmother is asleep in the next room. Don't rush your words. Speak clearly. **Your words** are only a small piece of the pie, but can make or break the conversation. Use simple language. Explain everything with honesty. Don't lie or try to bend the truth. Use good manners and greetings. Be mindful of the rhythm, speed, volume and pitch of your communication.

Be aware of **your non-verbal body language.** Look at what you wear. Is it neat or messy? Don't cross legs or arms. Be open. In person, maintain eye contact. Never take a call or attend to another task when you are with somebody. Focus only on the person, call or task on front of you. If the person talking to you has a negative tone, maybe they have a good reason. Maybe they got a bad product or poor service. That is their tone and their right to be how they are. Let this give you more reason to be professional and do all you can to communicate in a positive tone.

86. Respect their response

How it works

When I asked my editor, Managing Director of Book Hub Publishing, Niall MacGiolla Bhuí, which was his favourite part of *The Binman's Guide to Marketing*, he responded with one line from the chapter called, 'Go Door To Door'. I wrote, *'Respect their response'*. When Niall said this I thought, wow! If you don't read anything else just remember one thing: **Respect their response**. Customer service is about respect. Shep Hyken, one of today's leading experts on customer service, writes, *'Excellence comes out of respect, which is at the heart of customer service. It starts with internal service; treating the employees with the same respect and attitude as you would want the customer treated'*.

What to do

This is all about going back to basic good manners such as saying *'please'* and *'thank you'*. Make eye contact and display positive body language. If the interaction is in person address people by their name. Start with the basics and make sure you and your team are respectful, then you have a positive culture to build on. Then you can learn what communications best serve your customers. To respect the response of the customer you must learn to listen actively and let your actions be based on what they tell you. You must accept their reply. You don't have to agree with them. It may be an impossible request or their expectations may be a little different than your offering. For a solution to be reached you need to learn to accept the response. The best way to accept a response is to say, *'Thank you for sharing,* 'or *'Thank you for letting me know'*.

I learned this many years ago doing door to door sales with The City Bin Co. After presenting the sales pitch of the company as best as I could, I found that everybody would react differently to me. Many would sign up but those who didn't would give me a soft 'No' or a colourful rant. No matter what the case, I would always respond respectfully. When I was working in the call centre at The City Bin Co. the same principle applied. The root of this behaviour was the culture in the office. Simple good manners and people being polite and courteous. When you listen with respect and accept the response, you will usually get the same back.

87. Put your hands up

How it works

If you mess up, put your hands up. Take responsibility and own the situation. Fix it and make right, whatever is wrong. Too often, when we see something that is wrong, or a part of our service that is not going to plan, the easiest thing to do is to put it on the long finger and deal with it later. In most cases it will get pushed down the road and will not happen. Not all services and products are delivered perfectly for one reason or another and there can be hiccups in the customer journey. This is the moment where you can wow a customer. When you fix something for them and turn their bad experience into an amazing one.

On the 1st of January 2018, I bought a twin pair of M-Audio BX5 speakers for my music studio on Amazon. They arrived within a week. I was so excited. I was like a kid on Christmas morning waiting to open the presents from Santa. My smile turned sour when I realised there was only one speaker in the box. After consulting my order page to confirm the order was completed and speaking to the courier company, I concluded that there was an error made on their side. I ordered and paid for two speakers and they delivered only one. The speakers can also be bought separately. I used Twitter to contact their customer care team to explain what happened. A member of their team called me directly and apologised for the mix up. They sent the correct order of two speakers and told me to keep the single speaker free of charge. The problem was solved so fast and without a fight. I was impressed how quick it was resolved and the ownership of the problem by the customer care agent. In many big companies this is not the case as there can be a lot of hoops to jump through to get a resolution.

What to do

Firstly, it's fair to say not all customers are correct. There are people who will try to pull a 'fast one'. There are sometimes facts to say, you as a company, did something right. I am not talking about those cases. I am talking about when it's a fact that you messed up for one reason or another. Never ignore an issue or request from a customer because you simply don't know what to do. Don't deny it or make excuses. The best way to undo a bad service or mess up is to own up and say, *'You are right, please let me fix it'*. Put systems and values in place that allow your staff to resolve problems on the frontline.

There is nothing worst then when a hotel receptionist has to ask permission from her supervisor for every step she takes. That's not empowerment. At The City Bin Co., we keep it simple. Our brand promise means that if we don't deliver the service as promised the customer does not pay. This puts the spotlight back on us to perform to our best. Acknowledge there was a mistake if there is one and commit to resolving it. Understand that the customer is a person and is asking for help. That is your responsibility. Once the problem is fixed make sure to learn from it. Implement the right steps so it doesn't happen again. What happens when you ignore a mess up or hope it will go away?

When nine months of calls and emails to United Airlines failed to get Dave Carroll a resolution for the $1,200 worth of damage to his guitar caused by baggage handlers with their company, he did the one thing he knew how to do well; he wrote a song. It was called *United Breaks Guitars*. Carroll posted the incredibly creative and hilarious music video on YouTube, where the infectious tune went viral and today it has over 17 million views.

The Times of London reported at the time:*"...within four days of the song going online, the gathering thunderclouds of bad PR caused United Airlines' stock price to suffer a mid-flight stall, and it plunged by 10%, costing shareholders $180 million. Which, incidentally, would have bought Carroll more than 51,000 replacement guitars."*

As a company, design a clear and simple means of resolving issues that may arise. Brainstorm and roleplay with a handful of existing customers and go through all possible complaints and issues. Ask them to state which cases they feel are authentic and which are not. Discuss the best possible way to have a one-call fix that's a win-win solution for the customer and the company.

88. There is always a solution!

How it works

Imagine if you approach every situation with the idea that there is always a solution. And it's true; no matter what problem is in front of you there is always some kind of a solution. It's a frame of mind. This was the attitude I learned from my buddy and Sales Manager in The City Bin Co., James Kent. James has a knack for taking on big tasks and completing them with ease. When faced with a problem, he solves it methodically. When I asked James about his approach to all the different customer calls and sales requests that land on his desk every day he answered with a smile. He said; *'Once you understand there is always a solution you can approach anything no matter how big and deal with it'.* The solution may not be always to the liking of you or the customer but once it releases whatever tension is there or solves a problem that allows all involved to move on, that is success. Attitude is everything when you are speaking to a customer. If they are presenting a problem or looking for answers the best way to start that conversation is *'There is always a solution and I am happy to work on this for you'.* It creates a sense of calm which directs all parties to relax and put their attention on getting to the right answers for the customer.

What to do

Solutions happen when you don't attach yourself to the outcome. Maybe you can help a customer by digging deep and making an extra effort, however maybe the solution is that the customer can't be helped and the solution is to communicate that in a compassionate way that allows everyone to take the next step. When confronted by a difficult problem or situation make a decision to view it as something that you need to confront head on and solve. You can look at situations and say this is pointless or this is a waste of time. That conclusive thought provides a solution saying that it's time to cut losses or discontinue with something. Sometimes when you think that there is no solution, you have to realise that, there is the solution; that whatever is on front of you has run it's course. Behavioural Scientist Steve Maraboli puts it nicely when he said; *"Sometimes problems don't require a solution to solve them; instead they require maturity to outgrow them".* Start by writing all possible results down on a piece of paper. Ask why is this a problem. Often, it can be something as simple as poor communication at the point of sale. The one thing to believe when faced by any problem is that there is always a solution!

Meet the
World Class Customer
Service Experts

When I started writing the first book I knew that I wanted as many interviews in the back of the book as possible. I knew that my tips and techniques, my ideas and inspirations that filled the pages were just my personal thoughts that I had formulated in my journey from the back of the bin truck to selling recycling containers. I wanted that. I wanted you to feel like you were having a really interesting and engaging chat about business with the guy who collected your trash. But there was something missing. It wasn't enough. I wanted the book to be different. I wanted you to also sit down and have the customer service chat and be inspired by the best businesses that I have come across in my globe trotting. I learned from the first book that this was an amazing source of knowledge, to have a peep into other businesses in different industries and learn from them. For this book, nothing changes. I stuck with the same formula of asking a few on-topic questions that would help anybody with an interest in providing amazing customer service. I reached out to experts, business owners and mentors across the world and asked them for their take on the topic of the book and using their experience and know-how to give an even bigger inspiration to you on what is happening in the field of customer service excellence today.

Think of these interviews as if you are actually sitting across from that CEO, or customer service representative and having a coffee with them as they fill you in with their winning formulas on getting it bang on right. Imagine if you could travel across the globe and talk to people about customer service in Canada, Ireland, Ukraine, Poland, UK, South Korea, U.A.E and many other countries. That is exactly what you got here with interviews from different countries and different industries. From the Rotana hotel chain in the Middle East to Growing City, an award-winning recycling company in Canada. These are all companies that I have had first hand contact with, experienced their service and met with their owners. There are small companies with up to two employees and sole trader business owners and on the other scale there are large multinationals with a high number of employees. To learn to be a world-class customer service expert you need to be an amazing listener. You will discover that they nearly all speak the universal language of listening, walking in the customer's shoes, respecting the response and following up. You must listen to your customer, recognise their needs, tackle their concerns and understand why they are doing business with you. I certainly feel enriched with so much knowledge after conducting these insightful interviews. I hope you enjoy reading them and get as much out of them as I did.

89. Meet Chipright

Kevin Keane | Co-Founder & CEO | Ireland

Chipright is a strategic design consulting partner to companies in the semi-conductor market. They provide strategic consulting through experienced electronic engineers in the design and development of the latest generation of Integrated Circuits. These circuits appear in the Aerospace, Artificial Intelligence, Machine Learning, IoT, Automotive, Communication and Defense industries.

Question 1: *What are your top words to describe customer service?*

- Respect
- Honesty
- Transparency

Customers deserve your attention and **respect**. They deserve to be treated well and communication with them should be seen as open, **transparent** and **honest**. After all, good relationships are built upon those core values. Thus, if you value a good relationship with your customer – you should value the essential ingredients that form part of any good relationship. Anything else doesn't work. At Chipright, we have instilled these core values to be part of our business development program to stimulate forming good relationships with customers from the start of the engagement.

Question 2: *What is your number one method to wow customers?*

Firstly, at least deliver on what you said you would do. If you are capable to go beyond that and deliver your goods or services more efficiently and competitively, you will impress them and they may keep you on board. However, if you create a **customer care program**, request the customers input into creating that program and have the ability to tailor the program so that it fits well with their organisation. They will value that you listened openly to them. **Value** is the keyword here as the roll out of that program will derive value to them as you are both working in the same direction, which is how you **WOW the customer**. Give them value and attention above what they actually expect. How often does a customer get to give feedback, which directly improves how the outside organisation delivers to them? How often do they see it implemented? At Chipright, we rolled out a customer care plan and went as far as selling the concept that 'we care' to our customers, which we do and it resulted in developing better relationships with our customers and ultimately more business for our organisation.

Question 3: *What are the key ingredients for providing a great customer experience?*

You must listen to your customer, understand their requirements, address their concerns and do your upmost to understand the item they are looking to solve or resolve, after all that's why they are engaged with you, isn't it?
In doing so, you must put yourself on their seat and attempt to think like them. Figure out what they value and from there figure out how you think they are likely to engage with you when you meet them. The keywords here being '**meet them**' as that is the best way to engage any customer.

When listening to a customer its okay if they deliver a negative message to you. That's really what you want to know, understand and get to the bottom of. It's important to not let that message hit you personally, rather it is something you should be able to gather and store in a safe place such that when you have time to review the constructive criticism you can turn the negative energy into positive energy. After all, it's positive energy you want to push out to any customer going forward. In any business to business engagement, we treat the positive news and negative news as news for Chipright. It should never affect the person in the company who received it in a personal way. Being able to work with that in mind makes it possible to be able to deliver a great customer experience.

Question 4: *What's your advice to somebody starting out in business to help them be more customer focused?*

Simply listen to your customer or potential customer. Be open minded and flexible when considering ways forward for your business. Their requirements will relate to a problem that needs to be solved. If you can manage to listen, engage and solve that problem for one customer, you are likely to find the same problem reflected in many more customers. Thus, getting your product or service right from the start after listening to a customer should see your solution replicated in more areas. At Chipright, we focus on '**right from the start**' as a core offering as part of our care program.

90. Meet The City Bin Co.

Gene Browne | CEO & Co-Founder | Ireland

The City Bin Co. was started in 1997 with one truck, two customers and four bins. And an idea that a company could be driven by amazing customer service. Fast-forward twenty-three years and that core purpose of delivering excellent customer experiences is still central to The City Bin Co. Today, the company service tens of thousands of businesses and homes in Ireland and have earned many notable awards along the way.

Question 1: *What are your top words to describe customer service?*

- Amazing Service
- Customers
- Culture
- Churn
- Job Done

Question 2: *What is your number one method to wow customers?*

To wow customers you have get the job done right, first time and every time. To do this you need to have the right people, systems and culture. When you get this part, you cannot sit back and relax. You have to always be prepared for changes in your industry, economy, growth, and the many internal and external factors that will influence your business.

Question 3: *What are the key ingredients for providing a great customer experience?*

- Grow the right team
- Expect the unexpected
- Deliver your amazing service every time
- Create a healthy culture
- Don't do drama

Question 4: *What's your advice to somebody starting out in business to help them be more customers focused?*

Show up on time, every time with your homework done. Know your product and know your customer. Always follow-up until that job is done. If the customer is not a good fit for your company, let them go.

91. Meet Growing City

Lisa Von Sturmer | CEO & Founder | Canada

Lisa launched Growing City, the first company to focus on corporate organics in North America. It installs sustainably made stainless steel bins in clients' offices and offers organics recycling services, as well as traditional in-office recycling. It was an immediate hit in Vancouver and in 2012 Von Sturmer decided to introduce Growing City to a larger audience by taking part in CBC's hit reality TV series Dragons' Den. Growing City prides itself on award-winning customer service and on being reliable.

Question 1: *What are your top words to describe customer service?*

- Responsive
- Solutions
- Follow-up
- Thoughtful

Question 2: *What is your number one method to wow customers?*

The key to excellent customer service is to always add value by addressing and solving your customer's problems. Whether it's connecting them to the proper resource or service type, our team is trained to quickly identify what the best solutions to a client's challenges are. We ensure that we offer value in every interaction. If our services aren't the best fit for a customer, then we recommend another provider who can better address their needs. Even if we don't end up working together in that moment, the customer will remember that we sincerely cared about helping them. People don't forget that. Often, those customers will send other leads our way, and many end up coming back to us and wanting to work together.

Question 3: *What are the key ingredients for providing a great customer experience?*

Proper time management is fundamental to providing an excellent customer experience. Your team needs to schedule to follow-up with clients after every interaction - how did the service they recommended go? Did the article they sent over address their questions? Is there anything else they can do to fully address the customer's challenges? Anyone can answer a question over the phone or email, but few remember to complete the follow-through afterwards and that's where your team can differentiate itself with exemplary customer service. Training your team on being thoughtful is also very important. Did your team send your recently married client a physical congratulations card in the mail? Does your team take notes on your CSR for client birthdays, family names, hobbies and likes or dislikes? Finding ways to thoughtfully recognize, acknowledge or celebrate your client's achievements and milestones is a fantastic way to make someone feel special. Introducing some old-fashioned practices like physical thank-you cards, sending flowers, and calling people to wish them well can be pretty refreshing these days. Whenever you can pleasantly surprise and delight your clients, you keep your business top of mind and strengthen your relationship with them.

Question 4: *What's your advice to somebody starting out in business to help them be more customer focused?*

It's important to focus more on creating value for your clients rather than getting the sale when you're first starting out in business. Nothing turns people off faster than a "hard sale" - particularly in North America. People can tell the difference when someone is trying to help them versus trying to "sell" them on something. If you can switch your goal to successfully solving the customer's problem, you'll come across a lot more likeable and you'll have a better time creating a genuine rapport with them. If people like you, they're much more likely to want to buy from you and to continue working with you. Your end goal is to create repeat customers because it's always more profitable to sell to existing customers than first-time buyers.

92. Meet MOTM Events

Bruce Henry | CEO & Founder | Ireland

MOTM Events started as a murder mystery themed dinner theatre and has blossomed into a full-service event and destination management agency. In 2019 Bruce launched his new gamification line of business that focuses on developing new and exciting team building activities that focus on challenge, achievement, connection, competition and feedback.

Question 1: *What are your top words to describe customer service?*

- Intention - Why do we do this? What is the purpose and what do we want to accomplish?

- Integrity - Honour your word. If you say you're going to reply to someone by a specific date, honour it.

- Professionalism - You're dealing with real people and real money. Be professional at all times and always be courteous.

- Gratitude - Acknowledge the amazing opportunity before you because tomorrow is not guaranteed.

Question 2: *What is your number one method to wow customers?*

I organise all events as if they were for a close family member or friends regardless of their size or monetary value. As a company, its our responsibility to be mindful of all the little details that really make an event special and we pride ourselves on the speed in which we reply to emails.

Question 3: *What are the key ingredients for providing a great customer experience?*

- Mindfulness - How would I feel if I was planning this event? Is this the best we can do?

- Respect - We're constantly conscious that our events are always a celebration and we only get one chance to impress. Respecting this is the case encourages us to always put our best foot forward.

- Going the extra mile - We're always looking for opportunities to impress our clients. Sometimes that involves including additional guests at no charge or offering a complimentary prosecco reception at no additional cost.

Question 4: *What's your advice to somebody starting out in business to help them be more customer focused?*

Always remember that as a business owner, you're ultimately responsible for the experience delivered to your customer so be proud and celebrate when things go right but in the event things go wrong, have the courage and integrity to take responsibility and make it right even if it costs you a little more. Owning your mistakes and not passing the buck goes a long way and often turns an angry customer into an understanding customer.

93. Meet Snap

Ronan Walsh | Centre Manager | Ireland

Ronan Walsh is an experienced Management Professional having worked across a range of industries and holds an MBA from NUI Galway. Snap are Ireland's leading Print and Design company offering a full suite of products and services to help businesses grow. Ronan has a keen interest in Customer Experience, Sales, Marketing, Operations, Process Improvement and Brand Awareness.

Question 1: *What are your top words to describe customer service?*

- Understanding
- Solution orientated
- Genuine care and interest

Question 2: *What is your number one method to wow customers?*

Do what you say you will do. Deliver on your promises.

Question 3: *What are the key ingredients for providing a great customer experience?*

You must put the customer at the centre of everything you do. When you add/change/alter a process view it from the customers point of view... how will the change effect the way they deal with your business. Build a solid relationship with your customers and view it a as partnership – success for them is success for you. Make customer experience the lifeblood of you business.

Question 4: *What's your advice to somebody starting out in business to help them be more customer focused?*

To quote Peter Drucker; *"The purpose of business is to create a customer. We often get focused on items that draw attention away from the essence of providing excellent customer service"*. Make the customer experience the centre of your business. When making decisions, from marketing to processes look at them from the customers point of view – How will it make the customer feel? Will the customer get it? Does it make it easier for the customer to do business with us? It also helps to ask them or get family/friends to test it out as 'mock' customers.

94. Meet StockTaking.ie

Patrick McDermott | Managing Director | Ireland

Patrick has built Stocktaking.ie into an award winning national business that employs over 40 people. They provide an outsourced stocktaking service where the focus is on the accuracy of stocktaking. His clients include retail, pharmacy and hospitality.

Question 1: *What are your top words to describe customer service?*

Communication is a two-way thing, **listen**, it's all about **people**

Question 2: *What is your number one method to wow customers?*

Consistency

As a business that thrives in delivering a professional stocktaking service, we are only as good as our last days work. If we screw up, we have to suck up and that's damaging to our brand promise. If we provide a consistent service to customers they will know that what we do is quality and that they then have confidence in the results we present to them.

Question 3: *What are the key ingredients for providing a great customer experience?*

We have been using the Net Promoter Score (NPS) as a tool for accurately measuring how we operate as a service business. We find it excellent for discovering issues in our service that may have gone unnoticed otherwise. Our customer retention has gone up as has the quality of feedback to our delivery teams. The communication loop between office - delivery team - customer - repeat, is crucial in delivering a high standard. I'm delighted to say that the service we provide for the past 12 months is 72 which is regarded as "world class".

Question 4: *What's your advice to somebody starting out in business to help them be more customer focused?*

Listen to what your customers are saying. What are their pain points? Then tweak and design your business to address their exact pain points.

95. Meet Steeltech Sheds

Sean Brett | Founder & CEO | Ireland

Sean Brett is a serial Entrepreneur and the Founder & CEO of Steeltech Sheds, a Garden Shed, Garage and Garden Room manufacturer. Sean believes a good work ethic, an open and creative mind along with a passion for delivering a great customer experience is the key to a running a thriving business.

Question 1: *What are your top words to describe customer service?*

- Always start with a **smile**

- **Friendliness**

- Have the ability to **listen**

- Always have **integrity**

Question 2: *What is your number one method to wow customers?*

- **Presentation:** Present both yourself and the product in the highest possible standard at all times

- Also, be **controversial**, be **outrageous** and **never be boring!**

Question 3: *What are the key ingredients for providing a great customer experience?*

- If you promise something, like a delivery date, ensure you meet that date (or even before that date!)

- Provide a "**Welcome Pack**" - Include the boring paperwork but add little gifts such as branded pens, key-rings and battery packs. We include branded Steeltech jackets that, in turn, allow the customer to market for us.

Question 4: What's your advice to somebody starting out in business to help them be more customer focused?

- Read **every Customer Service book** you can

- **Treat your customers** as well as your children

96. Meet OnepageCRM

Michael FitzGerald | CEO and Founder | Ireland

Michael FitzGerald's OnePageCRM is a platform that provides an easy but powerful sales application for small business. It converts leads to customers fast on a simple dashboard, and does it with a beautiful user experience.

Question 1: *What are your top words to describe customer service?*

I think of just one word to describe customer service. I think 'Opportunity'. An opportunity to shine in front of our customers, an opportunity to stand out from our competitors, an opportunity to sell. We're all selling, all of the time. Even our kids sell to us when they're looking for a treat. There's a huge opportunity to build a relationship and, ultimately, sell when a customer has an issue. While many companies see customer service as merely a cost centre, we use it as one of our primary sales channels. We shine when we're responsive, when we listen and when we show empathy. For the customer, it's an opportunity for them to "test our metal." In a way, asking us "Are you up for the challenge?"

Question 2: *What is your number one method to wow customers?*

Pick up the phone. For a low-cost product like ours, it's important to think of the long-term game. How often does a company *call* you when you're in trouble? When they want to sell to you, absolutely. But after the sale is done, they usually leave you to muddle through help sites, watch tutorials, ask colleagues. We like to surprise our customers with a call, offer a screenshare, do a customized video... go the distance! We choose customer support Zappos style. (What we call the effort Tony Hsieh made in Zappos to wow customers, as described in his book Delivering Happiness).

Question 3: *What are the key ingredients for providing a great customer experience?*

It has to come from the top. If your organisation's leader doesn't fully see the advantages and opportunities of a great customer experience, it's hard for others down the line to ultimately deliver it to the customer. It can't be just part of a documented process or procedure. Exceptional customer experience needs to be part of your company culture. As they say, culture eats strategy for breakfast. Culture also kicks process out of its way for customer support.

Your customer success team must be empowered. They need to be able to act immediately to fix an issue or respond to a query in appropriate time and over the best channel. They need to know that management is behind all they do for customers. What starts with respect for your support staff, will in turn lead to the right mix of care, empathy and understanding to build relationships with your customers.

Question 4: *What's your advice to somebody starting out in business to help them be more customer focused?*

Put the customer-centric mindset right there, at the pinnacle of the culture in your business. Yes, you'll be busy creating the widgets or whatever you do, but in the remaining time your focus should turn to listening to your current (and future) customers. The start-up needs to know the pain points of their prospects. And the only way to find them out is to ask the right questions... and listen. After you develop the habit of listening to product feedback at the early stages, convert that same empathy into customer support when you're actively selling into the marketplace. Get out of the office, go and meet your customers, put yourself in their shoes. And most of all - don't hide! Don't hide behind contact forms, FAQs or your support staff. Don't have a culture of protecting anyone from the customer inside the office. The CEO needs to know what the customers really think, whether they are happy or feel let down.

One of the funniest, and best, blog posts Seth Godin posted on customer service went like this... *Rules for treating inbound customer calls with respect: Spend a lot more money on this. Hire more agents. Train them better. Treat them with respect and they'll do the same to those they interact with. Have a bright red-light flash on the CEO's desk whenever anyone, anywhere, is on hold for more than 5 minutes. If it gets to seven, have the call automatically route to the mobile phone of the CEO's spouse.* This is a brilliant way to show your staff in a light-hearted way how serious you are about support.

97. Meet SiteMinder

Evy Perez | EMEA Service Desk Manager | Ireland

SiteMinder is the global hotel industry's leading guest acquisition platform, with 35,000 hotel customers. In 2018, its technology helped hotels to generate in excess of 87 million reservations worth over US$28 billion in revenue. Evy joined SiteMinder's Galway office in its earliest days to lead the support desk team, which, in an always-on business like SiteMinder, means they provide real-time phone, email and live chat support to the company's large customer base not only within EMEA, but oftentimes around the world. Prior to SiteMinder, Evy worked for Buy.com as part of their customer service and operations departments, and, before that, SAP and Wayfair.

Question 1: *What are your top words to describe customer service?*

Human comes to mind first and, at SiteMinder, our motto is to provide service that's fast, friendly and knowledgeable. For me personally, I'd say **honesty**, **quality** and **responsibly**. **Honesty** because in order to keep a customer happy, they need to trust you, to know that whatever you are doing or saying is only to help them do better. **Quality**, because customer service is about time, effort, and patience. We can't help or support a customer if we only spend a couple of minutes listening to what we think they need. The best service we can offer also comes with everything else you put into that call or meeting. **Responsibly**, because the moment we pick up the phone to hear about a customer's problem, it instantly becomes our responsibility to do whatever is in our hands to help that customer. Working with our colleagues to find the best solution is our responsibility, our first and main task.

Question 2: *What is your number one method to wow customers?*

Be honest, because your customers recognise authenticity and it instantly builds trust. In the absence of everything else, even if your product or service has flaws, you know you have their trust. Always be on top of everything they need. **Follow-up** with them to see that everything's okay, and be as efficient as possible when they need you. Sometimes it is not about what you have done for them, but how you made them feel, and **communication is key** here like in a romantic relationship. Customers like and deserve to know what is happening, even if nothing is happening at all.

Question 3: *What are the key ingredients for providing a great customer experience?*

In a customer service department, the first and most important ingredient is the people. If they don't feel a genuine need to help others, if they do not enjoy it, the customer will never be fully satisfied, even if that customer's problems get solved. *Adequate service doesn't necessarily equate to a great customer experience.*

Almost as important as having the **right people** is having the **right tools**, processes, systems and training in place. Customer service agents are first in line any time a customer needs help, advice and counsel, so they need to be armed to speak with confidence and knowledge.

Question 4: *What's your advice to somebody starting out in business to help them be more customer focused?*

Do not neglect your customer service department. They're the people on the frontline who are winning your customers over and over after the initial purchase, hearing them at their times of need and understanding their biggest fears and frustrations. Ensure you budget accordingly and **invest in your people** on the frontline.

Listen to what your customer service agents have to say and don't waste the precious insights they can give you about your customers and your business. You will learn more from them than you can imagine.

98. Meet Rotana Hotel Group

Guy Hutchinson | President & CEO | UAE

Rotana opened its first property, the Beach Rotana Abu Dhabi in 1993 and is today one of the leading hotel management companies within the Middle East, Africa, Eastern Europe and Turkey. Rotana combines a unique understanding of the service culture and communities of the Middle East with the collective expertise of an executive team contributing to years of international experience in the hotel and service industry.

Question 1: *What are your top words to describe customer service?*

Space, connectivity and quality. These are what I personally think customers are looking for when booking a hotel. Space is related to the actual size of the room and facilities. Whenever you go, and whatever hotel you are paying for, space makes all the difference. Space is also related to privacy and non-intrusion from 'over servicing' guests, which can be overwhelming at times, especially when it is not genuine. Connectivity is a crucial key component in our industry today. Guests want to be connected at all times, and with multiple devices, which is something that I personally ensure we have across all our hotels. Quality is a standard for us and wherever our guests chose to stay, quality in our product offering is key components in customer service. This is the value we offer our guests.

Question 2: *What is your number one method to wow customers?*

Recognition and discretion. Guests love to be recognised for their loyalty and/or their choice of selecting the hotel they are staying at, for whatever rate they are paying. Wowing them with the little gestures or the personal touches goes a long way, without intruding in their privacy.

Question 3: *What are the key ingredients for providing a great customer experience?*

Well experienced and empowered team members give guests the confidence and reassurance and this is a matter we focus greatly on with our employees. Today, guests are also looking to access unique offerings, whether food & beverage related, recreational, destination or health related and we like to ensure offering these experiences across all our hotels. Finally, value is an important matter we focus on by maintaining the right pricing, whether guests chose to stay at our Centro hotels, Rayhaan, Arjaan or Rotana Hotels & Resorts. It's satisfying to feel that you paid the right price for the right product!

Question 4: *What's your advice to somebody starting out in business to help them be more customer focused?*

Know your business, surround yourself with people who are continuously thinking about ways to improve the business and hear out what your customers want.

99. Meet Jammy Instruments
Maria Teplitskaya | Head of Customer Success | Ukraine

Jammy Instruments is a music tech company focused on designing innovative hardware and software solutions making music practice and creation mobile and accessible. Their product line includes Jammy Guitar, a digital backpack-size guitar with a detachable neck, that was successfully crowdfunded on Indiegogo, and won Best in Show Award at Summer NAMM 2018. With Jammy Guitar, they aim to provide the best option for both hobby guitarists looking for a full-fledged super-portable instrument to practice anywhere, and for music creators in search of quality and affordable stringed MIDI controller.

Question 1: *What are your top words to describe customer service?*

- Attentive
- Empathetic
- Solution-oriented
- Prompt
- Personalise

Question 2: *What is your number one method to wow customers?*

To exceed customer's expectations. It's great when you have some basic satisfaction tools such as free products or discounts to make your customers happier or send it out as an apology. But what can be better is to find an outstanding personalised solution your customer didn't expect to receive.

Once we were chatting with a customer who uses a wheelchair, and he said that while he really liked Jammy, our detachable frame was inconvenient for him. He shared his thoughts with us on what shape would suit him better, and we worked with our CAD designer to create a custom frame model for our customer to 3D-print.

Paying attention to inquiries and suggestions you receive from your customers is another vital thing to make a wow effect. We have a whole community of guitar players using Jammy, and they have a lot of great ideas we are happy to receive, collect, and implement. We always make sure that we pass their suggestions to our engineering team. Of course, we can't implement every great idea we receive from our rockers. However, we always let our product team know what our customers want. If we release any of the requested features, we follow-up with the users who were interested in those specific features. So they know that we hear them, remember them and keep working on the product for them. Sometimes we offer users to join our beta-testers group for new firmware or features. This way, they're not only getting a fresh update earlier but also take part in creating a product and improving it with us.

Question 3: *What are the key ingredients for providing a great customer experience?*

We could have started with naming the necessary things like product knowledge, relevance, helpfulness, empathy, promptness, etc. But it's too abstract and obvious, isn't it? Jammy Support Band is focused on delivering the best experience with Jammy Guitar as a new product and as a company. We pay attention not only to product support, providing our customers with basic and advanced technical support, but to user's expectations on the Jammy as well. Your customer's journey starts way before they have your products in their hands. It begins with information about your product, advertising, marketing, instructions, and knowledge base. Make it honest, clear, and useful. Our marketing team works hard to create correct expectations about the product, explain what kind of people it suits best, in what situations, etc. That's really important in terms of customer success because a distorted image of your product created by the advertising may lead to customer's disappointment. So, we're always trying not to be overpromising here to avoid the situation when expectations don't meet reality. Be honest. Sometimes you have to face the fact that your product just doesn't work as the user expected. If you can't make your product work for that customer, make your service work for them. If your user doesn't want to keep your product, make him or her keep good memories of your service and company.

Question 4: *What's your advice to somebody starting out in business to help them be more customer-focused?*

- Find out who your customers are and what they are expecting from your product.

- Try walking in your customer's shoes, and you will be amazed by the many things you didn't think of.

- Stay curious about why your customers behave the way they do, especially the unhappy or aggressive ones and you can turn haters into supporters.

- Create a detailed knowledge base, manual, and instruction.

- Create a customer support team which not only knows your product but loves it.

- Listen to your customers and remember, they are real people, with their own lives and tempos. Make communication with your support convenient for your customers in the first place.

- Follow-up with your customers when they expect, and especially when they don't.

100. Meet Infinity Jewellery & Gentleman

Yolanda & Enrique Ponce Dee | Owners | Spain

Brother and sister team, Yolanda and Enrique, are the owners of a high end jewellery and menswear boutique based in Jávea in Alicante, in Spain. A small and beautiful Spanish town that has a packed season of touristic visitors during the summer, but also has 53% of international residents all year round.

Question 1: *What are your top words to describe customer service?*

Customer service means, being interested in the people that visit us at our premises. We are always very keen on getting to know them. To know their story. We are committed to bringing to our boutique the latest and best quality jewellery and menswear so that people are willing to buy at our shop. But also, very much enjoy sharing conversation with our customers. Getting to know them. This relationship creates a great atmosphere where customers naturally feel comfortable and not only shop with us but, also enjoy their time-shared.

We always remember that we are also clients in other stores and are always interested in the person attending us, beyond our needs. We like to know little details about the people attending us, that allow us to get to know them. This is also a very nice part of the experience.

Question 2: *What is your number one method to wow customers?*

We always enjoy welcoming customers to our shop and asking them how their day is coming along. As we mentioned, we are a small hometown boutique and we are always happy when customers visit us. We find ourselves amused by how many customers are surprised or even thrilled by us being truly interested in them and not just giving them the general sales chat.

Question 3: *What are the key ingredients for providing a great customer experience?*

We are constantly working and improving our internal information processes. We are now four people working on different shifts. This means that maybe a customer will come and like some item, but not buy it right away. We take effort in transmitting the information to all our staff so that, when the customer returns, every employee knows what they liked; any special price offered, the size they needed, etc. All these details help us give a highly professional service and help us to get to know our clients tastes. In this way, they receive the impression that we are interested in them; in what they like, and that we respect any considerations other employee has had with them, regardless of who is attending them at any time.

Question 4: *What's your advice to somebody starting out in business to help them be more customer focused?*

Think about your goals and the company's goals and core mission of the company. Once you know where you want to be, in business terms, it is easy to establish the steps that will take you to you objective. And when this is clear, your day to day relationship with your customers and your suppliers will improve.

101. Meet Sound Republica

Terry Kim | Co-CEO | South Korea

With 22 years of business experience and a B.A. from Seoul National University and an MBA from Kellogg School of Management at Northwestern University Terry Co founded Sound Republica to distribute all genres of music from all over the world to more than 180 countries and almost 100 streaming stores. They not only distribute your music, but also create promotional content such as lyric videos and live performance videos, and specialises in social media marketing.

Question 1: *What are your top words to describe customer service?*

My top words would be "**understanding** what customers want, and providing what customers **need**."

Question 2: *What is your number one method to wow customers?*

To wow the customers, focus on their immediate wants. However, to build a long-term relationship with your customers and earn their trust, provide what they need, even though they don't realize the need.

Question 3: *What are the key ingredients for providing a great customer experience?*

- Frequent communication
- Thinking from the customer's standpoint
- Amicable attitude

Question 4: *What's your advice to somebody starting out in business to help them be more customer-focused?*

Become a customer yourself. There is no better way to understand the customers than being in their shoes.

102. Meet RX Music
Gina Arwish | CEO & Founder | Canada

RX Music is a consultancy service for experience-driven brands competing in a noisy global marketplace helping clients cut through noise to distill their signature sound, and curate distinctive music to create bespoke playlists, which are fine-tuned to the nuances of their brand, audience, culture, locality, and physical space. Established in 1999 with the mission of elevating the human experience, RX Music has contributed to captivating guest experiences in retail stores, restaurants and bars, hotels, spas, and many other environments.

Question 1: *What are your top words to describe customer service?*

One answer for everything: It's **Heart**.

Question 2: *What is your number one method to wow customers?*

Words, methods, ingredients, advice – regimen, aesthetic, principle, value, variable, whatever the descriptor is, whatever the input, it always comes back to, emanates from, and is forever the maxim that is **Heart**.

Question 3: *What are the key ingredients for providing a great customer experience?*

Heart should be at the forefront of how decisions are made considering and involving anything to do with running a business…managing people, resources – whatever it is.

Question 4: *What's your advice to somebody starting out in business to help them be more customer-focused?*

It's not lipservice. It's not said because it's fashionable or easy. It's the only way. It's all there is.

103. Meet Mediaplant

Chris Jones | Senior Account Manager | UK

Media Plant is a leading CD & DVD replication/duplication company based in Swindon, Wiltshire. Offering a range of services including, authoring, printing, packaging, order fulfillment, USB duplication, memory products, Video Brochures and much more. They are a customer focused company with strong beliefs in offering quality products and services.

Question 1: *What are your top words to describe customer service?*

- Excellence
- Focus
- Top priority
- Highest importance
- Number one

We have more customer facing staff than all the other departments put together.

Question 2: *What is your number one method to wow customers?*

Always provide great follow-up and excellent service with high quality product fairly priced.

Question 3: *What are the key ingredients for providing a great customer experience?*

The people we employ are of the highest calibre and have many years' experience in our industry giving them excellent all-round knowledge in our products. This is key. The people. The employees. If this is right the customer service will naturally follow resulting in happy clients.

Question 4: *What's your advice to somebody starting out in business to help them be more customer-focused?*

Put the customers' needs first each and every time.

104. Meet WMfono

Marek Gasior | Key Account Manager | Poland

Marek is one of the frontline heroes for WMFono, a Warsaw based pressing plant with 28 years of experience in optical media manufacturing and vinyl pressing. They specialise in premium quality CDs, DVDs, pure virgin vinyl providing individual and traditional approach as well as packaging and transport services. Their number one focus is the customer. Everything revolves around their customer.

Question 1: *What are your top words to describe customer service?*

These are just two: **Exceed expectations.**

Question 2: *What is your number one method to wow customers?*

I always try to think about an extra ordinary 'add on' (preferably not money related) to the usual product/service provided. In our unique factory @WMFono where vinyl is pressed manually, we invite our customer to take part in the actual production process by simply allowing him to press their very first record on his own!

Question 3: *What are the key ingredients for providing a great customer experience?*

- *Willingness*
- *Patience*
- *Passion*

Take a great dose of **willingness** and mix it with **patience** in proportions of 2:3 and add a pinch of **passion**.

Question 4: *What's your advice to somebody starting out in business to help them be more customer focused?*

The greatest challenge in becoming truly customer focused is to try to put yourself in the customer's own shoes, especially when things do not go as planned.

105. Meet Clares Flowers

Ciara Lawless | Owner | Ireland

Clares flowers has been running since the 90s, 1st shop was opened in Ballinasloe, West of Ireland in 1994. In 2012, Clares flowers expanded opening a second store in Banagher, Co. Offaly, providing flowers and floral design of all occasions with a focus on customer service and quality presentation.

Question 1: *What are your top words to describe customer service?*

Build product brand **loyalty**. Develop a **relationship** ensuring whom your providing a service /product is satisfied with the **service**. Set a sustainable **standard** of service that you can **improve** on overtime.

Question 2: *What is your number one method to wow customers?*

Ask them about what they like. **Help** them identify a need for the product/service you are offering. **Eye contact** is key when communicating in person. **Learn and know** everything about what your trying to sell and other conventional ways the product can be used or adapted. Provide customers with lots of **choice**. Take **pride** in your product and don't be afraid to take a step back and let the customer come to you. Have **patience.** Always remain leveled head.

Question 3: *What are the key ingredients for providing a great customer experience?*

By asking the customer for their feedback. You have to welcome both positive and negative. Focus on getting to know the community in which your business is established. For example, support another local business in the area, sponsor a local event or team. This will draw customers to your business.

Question 4: *What's your advice to somebody starting out in business to help them be more customer focused?*

Put yourself in the customers shoes and honestly ask is your product a need or a want. How you would like to be served? Strategise your marketing from that starting point.

106. Meet Nua Naturals

Hilary Foley | CEO | Ireland

Hilary is the force behind NUA Naturals, an organic health food company located in the west of Ireland serving the UK and European markets. The company is situated at the cutting edge of emerging global trends such as Gluten Free, Raw and Organic.

Question 1: *What are your top words to describe customer service?*

*Customer Service is the **backbone** of the **business***

Question 2: *What is your number one method to wow customers?*

Under **promise** & over **deliver** every time.

Question 3: *What are the key ingredients for providing a great customer experience?*

Contact, Contact, Contact. Keep the customer fully informed at every stage.

Question 4: *What's your advice to somebody starting out in business to help them be more customer focused?*

Put yourself in the customers shoes & give them what you would expect to get yourself.

107. Meet Creva Agri International

Noel Kelly | CEO | Ireland

Noel is an award winning international marketer who firmly believes that forging solid life long business partnerships is the route to great sales. Noel has facilitated B2B relationships across the globe for almost 20 years. An accomplished Dairy & Sales Farmer, Noel has a Dairy Farm and is the owner of two companies which have both witnessed triple digit growth in the last 5 years. At the core of everything Noel and his global team does is built around a love of Dairy and Positive Business Relationships.

Question 1: *What are your top words to describe customer service?*

- Be of **service** first, the business will follow
- **Listen** to the customer
- Anticipate your customer's **needs**
- **Share** your **knowledge** with the **customer**

Question 2: *What is your number one method to wow customers?*

Customer's look to us to solve their problems. We always follow-up to show our customers we are on their side and fighting in their corner. We believe there is no issue big or small that not can be solved. Our approach is that there is always a solution.

Question 3: *What are the key ingredients for providing a great customer experience?*

- Finding and minding the customer
- Don't make promises you can't keep
- Do exceed their expectations
- Be brilliant at communication with your customers

Question 4: *What's your advice to somebody starting out in business to help them be more customer focused?*

You must have an interest in the job you are doing to do an amazing job. **Respect your customers** like you would a good friend by taking an interest in what they do and what makes them happy as people.

Acknowledgements

Muchas gracias to my wonderful wife Eva, and my awesome children, Mani and Alana. Thank you to my brothers: Ronan, Parisch, Gene and my dad, Ray. Thank you to my Mother, who is not with us anymore, but continues to be a force to inspire me to do well and get things done with my many projects.

A special big thank you to Gene Browne, CEO of The City Bin Co. (and my brother!) for his support and belief in me.

Thank you to my editor and publisher Dr. Niall MacGiolla Bhuí and his team for their attention to detail and professionalism.

Thank you to Ray McDonnell for designing another super cool cover.

Thank you Shep Hyken for writing the beautiful foreword for this book.

Thank you to all the business people who gave me their time and wisdom for the interviews.

Thank you to Niall Killilea, Louise Niemann, and all The City Bin Co. staff and customers. Thank you to James Kent and the sales team at The City Bin Co.

Thank you to the super awesome authors and friends of the Book Hub Publishing family for their support.

About the Author

Oisín is passionate about smart selling, metric-focus marketing and providing amazing customer service. An internationally mobile business enthusiast, Oisín has worked in waste management in Europe and the Middle East.

Oisín's first two books *'The Binman's Guide to Selling'* and *'The Binman's Guide to Marketing'* are both Amazon bestsellers, and received international praises from top global business experts Marshall Goldsmith, Libby Gill, Verne Harnish, Jeffrey J.Fox, Al Ries and Dr Paddi Lund.

Oisín's intention is to write a series of business books that will guide, motivate and inspire business owners and their teams. This is the third book in the series focusing on 'Amazing Customer Service' and will be followed by many more!

Oisín's business learnings come from his time and experience in one of the most exciting and fastest growing companies in Ireland, The City Bin Co., an award-winning utility company based in Ireland. He works for The City Bin Co. as part of the sales, marketing and innovation team.

Oisín also worked as head of key account management for B2B in the UAE, Qatar and Oman for averda, the largest environmental solutions provider in the MENA region. He was involved in implementing the sales process, training the sales team and coaching the key account management team.

Oisín regularly gives keynote talks and workshops to businesses, business groups and business schools on selling, social media marketing, marketing, motivation and amazing customer service.

When Oisín is not too busy selling bins, and speaking about his journey, he enjoys writing songs and travelling between the West of Ireland & Spain.

www.oisinbrowne.com